For Michael and Stephen

Designed by Peter Sims
© Copyright 1969 by Spitfire Productions Ltd.
Published 1969 by Purnell.
Made and printed in Great Britain by Purnell & Sons Ltd.,
London and Paulton (Somerset).
SBN 361 01388 4

"Battle of Britain"

BY TOM HUTCHINSON

The true story of those dramatic
four months in 1940, illustrated with
photographs from the great
new motion picture

PURNELL
London W.1

CAST OF THE BATTLE OF BRITAIN

The British

Harry Andrews—Senior Civil Servant
Michael Caine—Squadron Leader Canfield
Trevor Howard—Air Vice Marshal Sir Keith Park, Air Officer Commanding No. 11 Fighter Group
Ian McShane—Andy, Sergeant pilot
Kenneth More—Station Commander Baker
Sir Laurence Olivier—Air Chief Marshal Sir Hugh Dowding, Air Officer Commanding-in-Chief, Fighter Command
Nigel Patrick—Group Captain Hope
Christopher Plummer—Squadron Leader Harvey
Sir Michael Redgrave—Air Vice Marshal Evill
Sir Ralph Richardson—British Minister in Switzerland
Robert Shaw—Squadron Leader Skipper
Patrick Wymark—Air Vice Marshal Trafford Leigh-Mallory, Air Officer Commanding No. 12 Fighter Group
Susannah York—W.A.A.F. Section Officer Maggie Harvey

The Germans

Karl Otto Alberty—Jeschonnek, Chief of Staff, Luftwaffe
Alexander Allerson—Major Brandt, Heinkel Bomber Wing Leader
Dietrich Frauboes—Milch, Inspector-General, Luftwaffe
Wolf Harnish—General Fink
Curt Jurgens—Baron Von Richter
Helmut Kircher—Boehm, Fighter pilot
Malte Petzel—Beppo Schmid, Colonel in Intelligence
Manfred Reddemann—Falke, Senior pilot
Hein Riess—Reichmarschall Herman Goering

"I have never accepted what many people have kindly said, namely that I inspired the nation. Their will was resolute and remorseless and, as it proved, unconquerable. It was the nation and the race dwelling all around the globe that had the lion's heart. I had the luck to be called upon to give the ROAR!"

Winston Churchill, 1954

FOREWORD

As you read the story of the Battle of Britain in the pages which follow, you will see in your mind's eye the Hurricanes and Spitfires diving down on the German bombers and their fighter escorts, all of them glinting in the sun as they twisted and turned against the bright blue of the sky. You will imagine that you can hear the rat-tat of machine-gun fire and see the long orange-coloured lines of tracer bullets criss-crossing the whole scene, adding colour to and competing with the vapour trails, and you will imagine many other things.

In doing so, do not forget that down on the earth below there were people whose faith, brains, eyes and hands made it possible for the "Few" to do what they did. They were the men and women of the Royal Air Force in the radar stations dotted around the coast who tracked the enemy aircraft coming in over the sea. They were the men of the Observer Corps, dotted about the countryside, tracking them over land. They were others of the R.A.F. who operated the radio and telephone networks, and those in the operations rooms who received all this information and passed it on to the pilots in the air. And on the airfields were the men who strove with might and main to keep the fighters fit to fly. All these people, and many more, were the "Many". They formed the shaft of the arrow. The "Few" provided the sharp end—the arrow-head. In all it was a great team, worthy of the great victory it won against a courageous and worthy enemy so that the door of freedom could be kept ajar until the day when it could be flung wide open again.

Tom G'Crane

Air Historian for the Battle of Britain Fighter Association

CONTENTS

BUILD·UP

The clouds were banked high as mountain peaks. And through one range of cloud came a heavy Heinkel bomber, loaded with bombs to drop on Britain. It hulked as ferocious as a bully about to beat up a smaller boy.

The Spitfire didn't hesitate for a moment. The pilot touched the "stick" and the plane dropped upon the bomber—a minnow attacking a whale.

Behind the safety-goggles the pilot's face was tense, his teeth set tight against the speed of his fall. But his machine guns were chattering, spraying bullets into the Heinkel.

From the Heinkel came an answering roar of bullets. The Spitfire moved nearer into the attack. Then from behind came the splatter of more gunfire . . .

A Messerschmitt fighter-plane, escort to the Heinkel, had moved in behind. The Spitfire seemed cornered.

But the Spitfire had one advantage that its pilot knew well how to use. It had a speed of 355 miles an hour—and it could turn more tightly than the Messerschmitt.

That's what it did. Turning straight up as though climbing an invisible wall, the Spitfire hurtled round to turn the tables on the Messerschmitt. The eight 0.303 inch Browning machine guns slammed their lead at the Messerschmitt.

A plume of smoke floated delicately away from the German plane. Then more Messerschmitts slid into the view of the Spitfire pilot. Too many! Better to live to fight another day!

The Spitfire streaked away . . . and down below on the green ground of South East England children watched and speculated among themselves:

"Bet it was a Hurricane."

"Nah . . . more likely a Spitfire."

For it was a time for heroes. Dogfights like these snarled above Britain in what was to be called the Battle of Britain. For this was the way war was being waged between Britain and Germany in the summer of 1940—in the air.

The Battle of Britain was the first and last battle fought in the skies —with no help from ground troops.

It was a battle that lasted over a period of sixteen weeks in 1940. It was at times bloody and terrible; but it also had its moments of chivalry and high courage.

At a time when wars were being waged by vast impersonal armies controlled—so it seemed at times—by remote control push-buttons, the Battle of Britain was often a fight between two men, each in their separate machines of destruction. So it became a deadly contest, a ferocious game, a conflict that was almost personal.

The pilots of both sides knew the names of some of their rivals. Rather in the same way that, later in the Second World War, Field Marshal Montgomery in his desert campaign used to keep a photograph of his deadly enemy, Rommel, in his caravan.

Adolf Galland and Werner Mölders were said to be the most deadly accurate of the German aces. The British had men like Douglas Bader, Bob Stanford Tuck, Ginger Lacey, Peter Townsend, Al Deere, Tom Gleave . . .

Royal Air Force blue was a colour to wear with pride. It was the colour of courage.

But why was this courage necessary? Why were young men of Germany and Britain killing each other in the skies above Britain? From what dreadful furnace had emerged the white-hot shape of battle?

We have to go back in time.

You could go back farther than June 28, 1919, but that date stands as the most sinister beacon to light the way to the Second World War. For on that date the Treaty of Versailles was signed, the legal ending of the First World War in which Germany had been brought to ignominious defeat.

The treaty imposed conditions upon Germany that were later considered too strict. At the time Marshal Foch, for the French, said with fantastic foresight: "This is not peace; it is an armistice for twenty years."

Germany looked for a chance to regain her strength and glory, to weave the shreds of her pride into a shining, bright new uniform. It was Adolf Hitler who became the most terrifying tailor that Germany and the world had ever known. The uniform was that of the Nazi Party and it was decorated by the crooked cross—the swastika.

To outsiders Adolf Hitler, with his strutting walk and his comic Charlie Chaplin moustache, might have seemed a bit of a comedian. After all he had only reached the rank of corporal in the German Army during the First World War . . . what kind of leader was this?

He was the kind of leader the Germans wanted. They took him seriously. The man who had been an Austrian and had then settled in Germany was to become one of the most ruthless dictators ever known.

His political party was the National Socialist German Workers' Party —the Nazi Party. And in the 1933 German elections it was victorious and Hitler was made Chancellor of all Germany, later becoming President.

He began to break the conditions of the German-hated Versailles Treaty one by one.

Two of the top British pilots who helped to win the Battle of Britain. Douglas Bader (left) and Ginger Lacey.

There was a riddle at the time that most of the children's comic papers ran at one time or another:

Question: Why are Hitler's promises like pie-crust?

Answer: Because they're so easily broken.

But it was no laughing matter, although some short-sighted people thought that Hitler was a good thing because he and Germany could stand against the dangers of Russian communism from the East. They were wrong.

Hitler had written a book. It was called simply *Mein Kampf*, or "My Struggle". In it, for all to read, he had set out his intentions and aims. Those aims looked very much as though he were out to conquer the world.

It was fair warning. But not many people took heed.

Against all the rules he began to rebuild the German Air Force—which, anyway, had been secretly putting itself together—into the mighty German Luftwaffe under Herman Goering. And then, in 1935, he ordered conscription into the armed forces for all young men.

The war machine had begun to roll. And the Fuehrer—that's what he was now known as—began to pull the levers that would send the machine over all the world.

In 1936 German troops took over the Rhineland, a demilitarised zone that was protective for France.

Two years later Hitler took over Austria and part of Czechoslovakia.

In the meantime, for three years between 1936 and 1939, civil war had been raging in Spain. All the Big Powers said they would keep out of it, in case the small gunpowder keg blew up the whole ammunition dump, and forced a world war.

But Hitler saw the Spanish Civil War as a way to try out new weapons and tactics. His pilots moved in as advisers and fighters with Franco's Air Force. There ace Adolf Galland fought with his notorious Condor Squadron.

And there a word was coined that was to sicken every decent person: Blitzkrieg—the combined assault of bombers, tanks and troops on a city or town, sometimes even areas that contained no troops. The artist Picasso painted a famous picture—called "Guernica"—that illustrated the agony of one such city.

Britain's Prime Minister, Neville Chamberlain, was a man who was always pictured carrying an umbrella. He has often been criticised for his policy of appeasement—trying to come to terms with Hitler and his savage conquest of the countries of Europe.

But Chamberlain at last realised that it was difficult to turn the other cheek to a maniac. On March 31, 1939, Britain joined France in a guarantee to defend Poland if attacked.

They were saying, in effect, to Hitler: thus far—and no farther.

But the German High Command had made a deal with Russia not to attack them, and felt itself to be safe from attack in that direction. And anyway, Hitler, because of Chamberlain's policy, didn't believe that Britain and France would really fight.

On September 1 Hitler invaded Poland, his divisions smashing all aside within a matter of days.

Chamberlain's umbrella was going to be poor protection against the rain of bombs that was about to fall.

BREAK·OUT

Sunday, September 3, 1939 was an exciting day for Britain.

If you had lived then you'd have had your ear glued to the radio. Because television was still just a flicker in the future. Radio was the quickest means of telling people what was happening.

Every fifteen minutes the radio announced: "Stand by for an announcement of national importance at 11.15." And, throughout the morning, people gathered around their radio sets . . . waiting.

At 11.15 the people of Britain heard Prime Minister Neville Chamberlain. He said:

"I am speaking to you from the Cabinet Room at No. 10 Downing Street. This morning the British Ambassador in Berlin handed the German Government a final note, stating that, unless we heard from them by eleven o'clock that they were prepared at once to withdraw their troops from Poland, a state of war would exist between us.

"I have to tell you now that no such undertaking has been received, and that consequently this country is at war with Germany."

And in London the sirens sounded!

It seemed as though the Germans were following through with real power the fact that war had been declared. The moan of the sirens—used to tell people that enemy bombers were approaching and to take cover in underground shelters—sounded terrifyingly sinister . . .

But the alert was soon over. And those who had taken cover laughed themselves out of the shelters when they were told that the sirens had sounded because a single Allied plane had crossed the South Coast—without identifying itself.

Joke it might be. But it was a grim foretaste of what was going to happen to London in the months to come.

But only fortune-tellers can glimpse the future—and they were keeping rather quiet.

So the men, women and children of Britain went about their business, whistling hit songs like "Begin The Beguine" and grumbling at the blackout, when no lights were allowed to shine out on to the streets because they might give a clue to enemy aircraft.

That siren-for-nothing was a symbol of what followed in the winter of 1939/40 in Britain. That time was known as the "Phoney War" among the British who felt that nothing much was happening at all . . . people were bored and a bit apprehensive.

In the streets of British cities and towns you wouldn't have seen much evidence of a country at war. Sandbags appeared around public buildings as some kind of puny defence. The newly-created air raid wardens made themselves—people said—a nuisance by enforcing the blackout regulations and shouting, whenever they saw a chink of light at night:

"Put that light out!"

Everybody was disappointed that the Americans, in November, declared themselves to be neutral, but British success in their pursuit of the German pocket battleship *Graf Spee* outside Montevideo made the British cheer up a bit. That was on December 17—a pleasant Christmas present!

Russia had invaded Finland in November . . . but it all seemed so far away. And the British Expeditionary Force over in France settled in for a boring winter.

The Government decided that food should be rationed, so that everyone had an equal share and there was no excess profiteering as there had been in the 1914–18 war. In January, 1940, ration books were introduced for sugar, bacon, ham, butter and margarine. But children could still cheer—sweets weren't rationed until 1942.

It was a lull that couldn't last. And it didn't!

Poland had fallen. The Germans felt that they had waited long enough. Their next move, on April 9, 1940, was to invade Denmark and then Norway.

For the first time it was apparent just how strong was the German Luftwaffe's command of the air. Although the Allies soon lost their air cover from *their* combat planes, such as the Gladiators, the Germans quickly seized airfields in southern Norway from which to protect their invading troops, and the tiny R.A.F. fighter force was as quickly driven out.

The 'umbrella' of air power was tremendously effective in helping the German army as it rolled onwards. Nothing could stop them . . .

France—an airfield about to be attacked by the Germans; the ground crew start to destroy the aircraft.

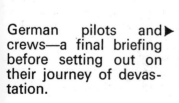

German pilots and ▶ crews—a final briefing before setting out on their journey of devastation.

On May 10 German tanks moved across the frontiers of Holland, Belgium and Luxembourg. The Nazis were flooding over Europe, and Europe was drowning.

But something else important happened on May 10. After a much-criticized reign as Prime Minister, Neville Chamberlain resigned. His successor was Winston Spencer Churchill.

The change was important for Britain in that here was one man who was capable of inspiring a bored, rather frightened people. People who didn't know what was going to happen next. Churchill told them.

On May 13, the same day that the Dutch Royal Family fled from a conquered Holland to Britain, Churchill said in the House of Commons: "I would say to the House, as I said to those who have joined this Government, 'I have nothing to offer but blood, toil, tears and sweat . . .'

". . . But I take up my task with buoyancy and hope. I feel sure that our cause will not be suffered to fail among men. At this time I feel entitled to claim the aid of all and I say 'Come then, let us go forward together with our united strength.' "

It still seemed to be a bit like whistling in the dark; shouting loudly to pretend you're not scared.

For a while the British defiantly sang "We're Going to Hang Out The Washing On The Siegfried Line" . . . the Germans were still advancing; their Luftwaffe was smashing a way through for the ground troops.

Churchill had made the controversial Lord Beaverbrook Minister of Aircraft Production—to cut through red tape to get the planes prepared, because the High Command realised that the war was going to be in the air. That was how the Germans had won so far. Soften their victim up first—then march in singing their song of triumph.

Their song of triumph was swelling now into a mighty chorus! The Germans had hacked their way into France, and on May 23 General Alan Brooke wrote in his diary: "Nothing but a miracle can save the British Expeditionary Force now and the end cannot be very far off."

Two days later the "miracle" began . . . the "Miracle of Dunkirk".

They called it a "miracle" because 224,585 British and 112,546 French and Belgian troops were brought from off the beaches of Dunkirk. A staggering number for a defeated army. But the retreat was accomplished between May 25 and June 4 by 222 naval ships and 665 other vessels.

Many brave private citizens took their own boats over the English Channel, which was sown with mines like so much explosive seed.

One man, for instance, was a retired Naval Commander, C. H. Lightoller, D.S.C., who sailed his yacht *Sundowner* from Ramsgate. Before the war the yacht had never carried more than 21 people on board. Braving the mines and the bombs the *Sundowner* came back to Britain with 130 troops on board!

Flying ace Douglas Bader remembers that Churchill ordered a last patrol over the Dunkirk beaches on June 4. The crumbling town lay under smoke. Out of the harbour sailed a single yacht with a little white sail. "It must have been the last boat out of Dunkirk."

The R.A.F. pilots circled it protectively until low petrol forced them to turn for home.

16

▶

"I have nothing to offer but blood, toil, tears and sweat . . ."—Winston Churchill. A poster (right) of Churchill exhorting the British to be united in their battle.

"LET US GO FORWARD TOGETHER"

Bader remembers it as one of his most vivid memories of the war.

The Army left behind a good deal of heavy military equipment. The British position seemed hopeless. But there was to be no surrender.

The Germans looked longingly across that 22-mile-wide stumbling-block of water known as the English Channel. So near and yet so far! And they cheered when on June 4 Hitler signed a War Directive.

This read: "As England, in spite of her hopeless military position, has so far shown herself unwilling to come to any compromise I have decided to begin preparations for and, if necessary, to carry out the invasion of England."

On that day, too, Churchill was saying in the House of Commons: "We shall go on to the end, we shall fight in France, we shall fight on the seas and oceans, we shall fight with growing confidence and growing strength in the air, we shall defend our island whatever the cost may be, we shall fight on the beaches, we shall fight on the landing grounds, we shall fight in the fields and in the streets, we shall fight in the hills; we shall never surrender."

That was Britain's answer to the Nazis.

On June 10 the Fascist state of Italy joined Hitler—and declared war upon Britain.

With France toppling like a pack of cards and Paris occupied, Churchill growled on June 18: "What General Weygand called the Battle of France is over; the Battle of Britain is about to begin."

In reality what has become known as the Battle of Britain began on July 10 as the Luftwaffe went into Phase One of Germany's plan of attack by attacking Britain's coastal shipping.

Britain's position looked hopeless to the outside world. British soil was not safe. (Even as early as November 1939 bombs had been dropped on the Shetlands—the first to land on Britain.)

People prayed or crossed their fingers. But if they'd looked for it there was one fact that was a weather-vane to show the way the wind would blow in the future.

At the time of Dunkirk over a period of four days the Royal Air Force had shot down well over 150 Nazi aircraft. The R.A.F. had only lost twenty-nine.

With that kind of courage the odds might yet be evened up . . . for a country whose position was said to be "hopeless".

▶
The Germans, having been joined by Italy, invade France.

INTO BATTLE

You've seen it happen many times on the cinema-screen. The moment in a cowboy film when everything looks hopeless for the forces of law and order.

The hero and/or heroine about to be shot/burned at the stake/lynched/or otherwise suffer grievous bodily harm when up rides the Cavalry—to the rescue.

The audience reach for their hats, knowing that once again right has triumphed and tyranny has been overthrown.

The trouble is real life has little to do with Western films.

And so it was with Britain in 1940.

There was no cavalry to ride to the rescue. The rest of the world that was not conquered by Germany might look on sympathetically like the Americans, but, like the Americans, they remained neutral.

True, the first squadron of the Royal Canadian Air Force arrived in Britain to help the British Fighter Command but the simple fact remained: Britain was outnumbered. And completely alone.

It was like David waiting for the giant Goliath to advance upon him. But, like David, Britain had a sling. That sling was R.A.F. Fighter Command . . .

Admittedly, an outnumbered Royal Air Force. The R.A.F. had 600 serviceable fighters when the battle began, whereas the Luftwaffe had built up its fighter and bomber planes over the years to a staggering total of 2,500.

And yet . . . such was the remarkable stupidity (or was it courage?) of the British that, according to a Gallup Poll on June 22, 1940, only three per cent of the British population believed that the war might be lost.

How much more realistic was America where thirty-three per cent thought Britain's future was doubtful! But what was this? Thirty-two per cent believed in Britain's victory. And that on the same day that France submitted to an ignominious armistice with Germany! That "stupidity" was spreading.

Hitler, however, was not quite so certain as all that. In *Mein Kampf* he had talked with some respect about the British and what they were capable of if it came to fighting.

Now his High Command officers told him that daylight superiority in the air was essential before his troops invaded the British Isles.

"Britain is not our natural enemy," said Hitler and he sent peace offers via neutral Switzerland to Britain.

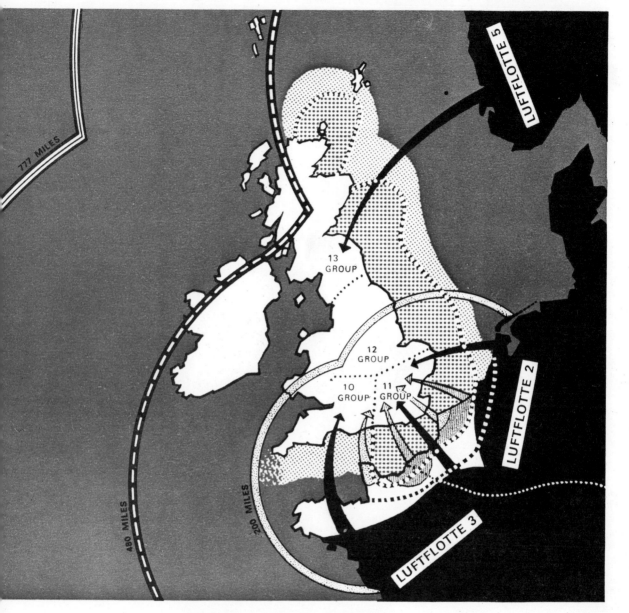

777 MILES

480 MILES

200 MILES

LUFTFLOTTE 5

LUFTFLOTTE 2

LUFTFLOTTE 3

13 GROUP

12 GROUP

10 GROUP

11 GROUP

DISPOSITION OF FORCES

n radar coverage 15,000 ft.	Enemy aircraft ranges	Luftwaffe base areas

September 1939

September 1940

Long range bombers

Long range fighters

Messerschmitt 109 fighters

Fighters

Stuka Dive bombers

Long range bombers

main German strike force was contained in
flotte 2 supported by Luftflotte 3 in the west and
lesser degree by Luftflotte 5 in Norway. On the
ish side Nos. 11 and 12 Fighter Groups bore the
t of the fighting although individual squadrons

were rotated for rest periods to the other Fighter
Groups over the 4 month period of the Battle, so
that the burden was evenly shared throughout the
whole Command.

ATT

ACK!

On July 16 he signed a further directive putting into plan-form the invasion of Britain. The invasion was to be called Operation Sealion.

Three days later, Hitler, hands clenched with passion, declared his "honourable intentions" towards Britain.

". . . I feel it to be my duty before my own conscience to appeal once more to reason and commonsense, to Great Britain as much as elsewhere . . . I consider myself in a position to make this appeal, since I am not the vanquished seeking favours, but the victor speaking the name of reason. I can see no reason why this war must go on."

Hitler had spoken of "guarantees". But the conquered countries of Austria, Czechoslovakia, Poland, Norway, Denmark, the Low Countries, France . . . knew what Hitler's guarantees were worth.

So did Churchill. So did Britain. On July 23 Britain contemptuously rejected Hitler's peace terms.

It seemed a foolhardy thing to do. Massed in Europe were the three Luftflotten (air fleets), already pouncing upon British shipping. Britain had the Royal Air Force.

Hitler realised that the R.A.F. Fighter Command had to be torn down from the skies otherwise his troops could not cross the English Channel and land in sufficient numbers to make it worthwhile.

Said Paul Baudouin, the French Foreign Minister: ". . . if the Germans do not master England this autumn they will have lost the war."

The war in the air was going to be crucial.

You can pinpoint the two combatants—the Luftwaffe and the R.A.F.—in two men: Reichmarschall Herman Goering, in overall charge of the German air force, and Air Chief Marshal Hugh Dowding, Commander-in-Chief R.A.F. Fighter Command.

Goering was fat, jovial and ferocious, a World War One fighter ace who was bloated now with power as well as poundage. He knew that the Luftwaffe was a masterful weapon, because he had created it.

Dowding in control of all air defence—including Anti-aircraft Command, Balloon Command and the Royal Observer Corps—was a very different kind of man.

He was lean, quiet, and never used one word where silence would do. He had been at Fighter Command since 1936 and was known as "Stuffy" because of his reserve.

But from his headquarters at Bentley Priory, at Stanmore, north of London, he had fought with politicians and had managed to build up as well as he could a Fighter Command that might be small, but which he knew was charged with courage and the spirit of the service.

How had he fought? After a long struggle he managed to get concrete runways for some of his airfields—hitherto they were of the more easily-camouflageable grass.

And he had created a flexible system of defence. In easily-attacked Southern England, for instance, fighter planes could be ordered from one group to another by operations-rooms communicating by telephone and teleprinter.

Look at the map (p. 25) and you'll see that the major group most vulnerable to attack was No. 11 Group in the South East. This was commanded by Air Vice Marshal Keith Park, a New Zealander. Backing up that Group was No. 12 Group, in the charge of Air Vice

Marshal Trafford Leigh-Mallory. Dowding's system of command meant that each Group was split into sectors.

There was also another weapon: radar. Radar is a commonplace word now. It was created by an R.A.F. scientific adviser Robert Watson-Watt and it was a radio means of locating enemy aircraft via three-hundred-foot-tall masts built along the coasts of Britain.

The Germans knew about radar, but discounted its real effectiveness in times of war. Dowding believed in its effectiveness—and he knew how to write a letter at the right time.

Now flashback to May 16, when France was fighting for its life. Britain was helping by sending its Hurricane fighter planes to Northern France, even though it all looked hopeless. Dowding thought no more British planes should be sent. He sent that letter.

The words are starched in stiff phrases but they're worth reading—especially that last paragraph of defiance.

"I believe that, if an adequate fighter force is kept in this country, if the fleet remains in being, and if Home Forces are suitably organised to resist invasion, we should be able to carry on the war single handed for some time if not indefinitely. But if the Home Defence Force is drained away in desperate attempts to remedy the situation in France, defeat in France will involve the final, complete and irremediable defeat of this country."

Defiance—and a warning. No more fighters were sent to France.

That fact, and the pause while Hitler tried his "appeal to reason", gave Dowding and his men a breathing-space.

May 16, 1940

Sir,

I have the honour to refer to the very serious calls which have recently been made upon the Home Defence Fighter Units in an attempt to stem the German invasion on the Continent.

2.   I hope and believe that our Armies may yet be victorious in France and Belgium, but we have to face the possibility that they may be defeated.

3.   In this case I presume that there is no-one who will deny that England should fight on, even though the remainder of the Continent of Europe is dominated by the Germans.

4.   For this purpose it is necessary to retain some minimum fighter strength in this country and I must request that the Air Council will inform me what they consider this minimum strength to be, in order that I may make my dispositions accordingly.

5.   I would remind the Air Council that the last estimate which they made as to the force necessary to defend this country was 52 Squadrons, and my strength has now been reduced to the equivalent of 36 Squadrons.

6.   Once a decision has been reached as to the limit on which the Air Council and the Cabinet are prepared to stake the existence of the country, it should be made clear to the Allied Commanders on the Continent that not a single aeroplane from Fighter Command beyond the limit will be sent across the Channel, no matter how desperate the situation may become.

7.   It will, of course, be remembered that the estimate of 52 Squadrons was based on the assumption that the attack would come from the eastwards except in so far as the defences might be outflanked in flight. We have now to face the possibility that attacks may come from Spain or even from the North coast of France. The result is that our line is very much extended at the same time as our resources are reduced.

8.   I must point out that within the last few days the equivalent of 10 Squadrons have been sent to France, that the Hurricane Squadrons remaining in this country are seriously depleted, and that the more Squadrons which are sent to France the higher will be the wastage and the more insistent the demands for reinforcements.

9.   I must therefore request that as a matter of paramount urgency the Air Ministry will consider and decide what level of strength is to be left to the Fighter Command for the defences of this country, and will assure me that when this level has been reached, not one fighter will be sent across the Channel however urgent and insistent the appeals for help may be.

10.   I believe that, if an adequate fighter force is kept in this country, if the fleet remains in being, and if Home Forces are suitably organised to resist invasion, we should be able to carry on the war single handed for some time, if not indefinitely. But, if the Home Defence Force is drained away in desperate attempts to remedy the situation in France, defeat in France will involve the final, complete and irremediable defeat of this country.

I have the honour to be,
Sir,
Your obedient Servant,

H.C.T. Dowding.

Air Chief Marshal,
Air Officer Commanding-in-Chief,
Fighter Command, Royal Air Force.

When the battle began there were almost 1,000 R.A.F. day fighter pilots available, 460 for the Hurricanes and 325 for the Spitfires. That was all.

And Operation Sealion was now planned for September 15.

Churchill was later to say of those pilots: "Never in the field of human conflict was so much owed by so many to so few."

The Few . . . were later described as "the gayest company who ever fired a shot in anger".

But, although the Few were the heroes, the front-line commandoes as it were of Britain's defence, everybody in Britain was sooner or later drawn into the conflict, like the sinews tightening in a clenching muscle.

There were, of course, the women of the Royal Air Force, the Women's Auxiliary Air Force. The men of the Anti-Aircraft Command. Balloon Command. The Merchant Navy. Coastal Command. Bomber Command.

The men of the Royal Observer Corps used ordinary field-glasses— sometimes just their eyes—to spot enemy aircraft . . . news which was then fed into the communications machine that would let Fighter Command know.

And, of course, there were civilians. But theirs was a role that was to be more fully enacted later on in the Battle of Britain.

Phase One of the Battle began almost mildly in comparison with what was to come later. Convoys of ships in the Channel were mercilessly harried by bombers.

Then the Germans started to extend their claws to wound the radar stations and such airfields as Hawkinge.

The damage was being done.

On August 1 Hitler had said: ". . . I intend to intensify air and sea warfare against the English homeland." Although—perhaps still thinking he could do a deal with the British—he added: "I reserve to myself the right to decide on terror attacks as measures of reprisal."

In other words: there was to be no blitz . . . yet.

But there was terror, all right. Or perhaps the words "a composed panic" might best describe the feeling that many of those in High Command felt about the situation.

The convoy attacks and the smashing up of airfields were continuing. The outnumbered Fighter Command was losing air fast.

On July 4 a radio reporter, Charles Gardner, had described a dog-fight over Dover as though it were a game:

"Oh, boy! Look at them going. And look how the Messerschmitts— oh that is really grand . . . I've never seen anything so good as this . . . the R.A.F. fighter boys have really got these boys taped!"

Now, as August advanced, the play was over. This was for real. It was as though somebody playing a game of cricket had discovered that the ball is really a hand-grenade!

And *Adler Tag* was yet to come.

Adler Tag? Eagle Day.

The day when the Nazis planned their biggest air assault yet upon British airfields.

The Luftwaffe-eagle stirred in its nest of Europe and prepared to launch itself—at Britain.

◄

The historic letter (left), sent by Air Chief Marshal Sir Hugh Dowding, which was instrumental in the defence of Britain.

THE HUN IN THE SUN

Overhead the heavy drone of bombers. Hear the thrum-thrum-thrum sound of them. Inside your flying tunic, which you haven't been able to take off since the last battle, you're hot and sweaty and you'd like to sleep . . . but the airfield siren screams at you that you've got to get your fighter up again—even though it's hardly refuelled.

You can't grumble. You're a pilot. A fighter pilot. And it's your job. Jerry is out to break up your airfields; to smash those springboards from which Britain's defence springs.

You're that defence. You're a pilot.

They wrote popular, sentimental songs about the pilots like "Silver Wings In The Moonlight". They were thought of as a rather gay, casual collection. Individuals.

But you had to have discipline to put up the kind of fight that the fighter pilots were putting up at this time.

It was dirty work. Gritty, grimy and sweaty. And one of their biggest enemies was just plain old-fashioned fatigue. It seemed you were in the air, or slumped in a deck-chair waiting for the order to get up again, all the time.

"Scramble!" was the command to get up in the air. One pilot reported, humorously, that he it was who was scrambled.

The pilots didn't know it but they were living through what was later described as Phase Two of the Battle of Britain. And Eagle Day was part of that phase . . .

It was planned for around August 10. The biggest number of German planes would then smash at Britain.

Bad weather over the tenth and the eleventh made the German attacks comparatively discreet. And although Eagle Day, according to German records, is August 13, the Eagles started swooping the day before.

August 12, remember, is the "Glorious Twelfth" when grouse-shooting starts in Britain. When game is "bagged" by the hunters. Who said the Germans have no sense of humour?

The big attack was on six of the major radar stations. Five escaped with damage that was not as bad as was at first thought, but Ventnor on the Isle of Wight went completely "blind" and couldn't be repaired

for days. This was while British fighters were heavily engaged with a German attack at Portsmouth.

Portsmouth was one of the shrewdest raids of the Battle. Through a gap in the barrage balloons came a force of Stuka dive-bombers—heading for a harbour brimming with ships of all kinds.

Shrewd it might have been but the Stukas only hit a brewery!

At the end of the day the R.A.F. wondered what would happen if the Luftwaffe really concentrated all its attention on the radar stations and the fighter airfields. Manston airfield was out of action.

What were the figures? The Luftwaffe had lost thirty-one aircraft; the R.A.F. twenty-two.

But the Germans, in their writing-up of the casualties, claimed *all* the targets that had been attacked, even though, perhaps, little damage had been done. And they exaggerated the British fighter losses at sixty.

The British were usually rather more reticent about their claims of planes shot down than the Germans. It was the *quality* of the evidence reported by returning pilots that mattered. If you saw a plane crash, obviously that was counted. If you saw it just spin away out of sight another witness was needed to corroborate the kill.

But on Eagle Day—now reckoned to be August 13—total German air strength was reckoned at 2,550. Fighter Command could muster only 749 fighters.

The German attack wasn't as heavy as expected at first. A message from Goering putting-off operations until later in the day failed to get through to some German squadrons.

But, in the afternoon, Luftflotte II smashed at Kent and the Thames Estuary, and Luftflotte III fought with No. 10 Group over Hampshire, Dorset and Wiltshire.

Three airfields were badly hit—Eastchurch, Detling and Andover—but they weren't fighter airfields.

During the day the Germans made 1,485 sorties (a sortie is a flight by an aircraft) and badly hit a Spitfire factory at Castle Bromwich, near Birmingham.

Listen to one pilot (a Canadian):

"The air was filled with Nazi aircraft. There seemed to be thousands of Messerschmitts, Spitfires and Hurricanes all mixed up in a series of dogfights. The three Hurricanes which I was leading concentrated on the Messerschmitts.

"I saw the third pilot of my flight fire a long burst at a Messerschmitt. He broke away when only 25 yards from the German machine, which went streaming down towards the sea. But we did not see it crash into the water, so we have not claimed it as a victim."

This was going on at a height of 15,000 feet. Oil from damaged aircraft foamed through the air, at times blacking-out the windscreens of both hunters and hunted.

One man in a Hurricane was hit, felt his engine stop and fell out of the cockpit. He had been hit at 19,000 feet and he dropped for about 12,000 feet before his parachute opened! The speed of his fall tore off his helmet, flying boots and socks. And he lived.

Luck, courage, moments of chivalry and horror. British pilots who fell into the sea ("down in the drink" was the expression) tried to stay afloat wearing their "Mae Wests", even though they might be floundering in their parachutes.

Sometimes other fighters would circle the spot where a comrade had gone down, so that air/sea rescue launches could find the floating man.

One rescue was made by a young girl who put out to sea in a small canoe. She later got a medal.

German pilots in the Messerschmitt 109's carried inflatable dinghies. They needed them. After all the British were fighting over their own country; there was a chance of survival if they baled out. But the Germans, if they fell on the land were captured; if they landed in the sea they had to sink or swim. So they used dinghies.

Eagle Day ended in a flurry of feathers as the facts came home to roost. Eagle Day, from the German point of view, had been a failure.

The Germans had lost 45 planes. Fighter Command only 13.

But the Nazis were nothing if not optimistic. Between August 8 and 14, they said they had successfully attacked about 30 airfields and that they'd destroyed 300 British fighter planes.

Fact: they had knocked out only 100.

The wish, as they say, was father to the thought. Three hundred British fighter planes, if correct, was nearly half of British fighter strength. How long could Britain hold out under such a mauling wondered the Germans?

It was glorious weather for a fight. The best summer for years. Ginger Lacey, one of the highest scoring British aces, says that: "You were desperate for a bit of cloud. Because if you saw cloud you dived into it for a bit of cover. You hated the sun because it showed everyone where you were—it showed the Hun where you were.

"And if he came at you out of that sun you never had a chance. You were blinded by the light and didn't know where to fire next."

The Germans' main fire was next directed at the North East of Britain. They thought the main British fighter strength would have been drawn down South.

But Dowding had foreseen all this. He was always several steps ahead of the Luftwaffe. He had fighters up there—No. 13 Group who were waiting for such a chance as this.

The Germans came in from Scandinavia, fitted with extra fuel tanks. They expected little or no opposition.

From above, the Spitfires looked down at the massed Heinkels— without their covering Messerschmitts—and gloated. Then they dived upon the unsuspecting enemy.

The mass splintered, crumbled, finally broke. It was, said one pilot afterwards, "An astonishing treat for us."

For the Germans it was horrifying. They thought that British fighters had leaked away as though through a plug-hole. They hadn't foreseen this. But their Intelligence reports were always remarkably exaggerated.

For instance, a party of about half-a-dozen German prisoners of war was being driven through London, on the way to a prison camp. They looked about them, saw the houses standing, saw the shops open, and gaped with astonishment. For they had been told that Britain was tottering on its last legs like a boxer who is punch-drunk and just about to fall to the canvas.

The German Intelligence reports were often wrong. On August 15 Goering ordered no more attacks on radar stations as they couldn't be destroyed—even though Ventnor had taken such a beating. Goering was relying on Intelligence reports . . .

The Germans continued to pound away at the airfields and other coastal targets. It was such a constant rat-gnawing away at Fighter Command that would win before Operation Sealion, September 15 —the Germans thought.

And that was the way it looked, even to those who were on the side of the British. Manston airfield was badly bombed on August 19 and at Tangmere the pilots had to return, land and re-fuel their planes while being dive-bombed by the Germans! British Fighter Command was being weakened, like a patient needing blood. And the transfusion that was needed was young pilots.

In ten days, for instance, at this time Fighter Command had lost 154 experienced fighter pilots. But only 63 had been trained to replace them.

But those pilots there were were flying so well, so courageously that the *New York Times* wrote:

"It is too soon for forecasts, too soon to draw one's breath in hope, but not too soon to applaud the brilliant performance of an outnumbered force in holding the invaders at bay, foiling attempts to put ports, airfields and munitions works out of business, chasing the bombers away from London, successfully defending the island while at the same time taking a bold offensive in a hostile country.

"During these crucial days the quality and spirit of the Royal Air Force have been written into the great legend, this time not in earth or water but in the sky."

On that same day Churchill spoke, in Parliament, about "The Few".

And as the Battle of Britain mounted in intensity towards a crisis that was going to make or break Britain, people thought about those Few—those pilots.

Their battlefield was the sky, their frontline a cloud. Could nothing break them?

THE HEROES-
THE PILOTS

Do not despair
For Johnny-head-in-air.
He sleeps as sound
As Johnny underground

The poet John Pudney wrote that to celebrate the pilots, the front-line heroes of the Battle of Britain. They deserve that—and more.

Their trade was killing. But they could do it with a sense of the fitness of things and the knowledge that they were doing what no other fighter had ever been called on to do before.

The German pilots were, perhaps, as brave—as the greatest of their aces, Adolf Galland, said, they hated "that strip of water, the English Channel, which Goering called a river but in which you could drown so easily if your plane came down".

But they, schooled in Spain and in Europe, were professionals.

Goering sometimes invited *his* fighter aces to relax at his hunting lodge, Karinhall, in Prussia. Those invitations were not always liked because, while resting, the ace might have his score bettered by a rival.

When German ace Werner Mölders stayed for three days he per-suaded Goering to detain Galland there for three days as well. So that Galland couldn't get more Spitfires than him!

They were professionals. The British pilots had a quality of amateur-ishness about them. But they had a tremendous advantage in their fight. They were defending, along with Commonwealth pilots and pilots from conquered countries, the place they knew as home.

Douglas Bader said: "They were a good bunch, those pilots—young, light-hearted, prone to under-statement in order to hide their feel-ings . . . they took a dim view of those Germans warplanes with their Iron Crosses and their crooked swastikas flying over our island king-dom and dropping bombs.

"We learned to hate, though not so much as the few Czechs and Poles fighting with us who knew the uncivilised savagery of the Nazi occupation of their homelands."

Richard Hillary, the ace who was badly burned in one battle crash, wrote: "The fighter pilot's emotions are those of the duellist—cool, precise, impersonal. He is privileged to kill well.

38

"For if one must either kill or be killed, as now one must, it should, I feel, be done with dignity. Death should be given the setting it deserves; it should never be a pettiness; and for the fighter pilot it never can be."

Two different kinds of men—Bader, outgoing and forceful, making himself learn to walk on artificial legs, after losing his legs in an air crash in 1931. Hillary, quiet, artistic and a man who fought pain alone.

What bound them together? What made them heroes? Perhaps that will always be a mystery. All one can say is that courage was the common denominator of their lives fighting in the Battle of Britain, although they would laugh now at any suggestion of it.

"It was a job you had to do," said Ginger Lacey. "There was a comradeship, of course; you were all together, after all, on the brink of an abyss, so you had to stick together . . . but it was like chopping down trees. If you carried on chopping . . . you got them all down in the end. They shot *me* down nine times."

On his first day in combat on May 13, 1940 Lacey notched up his first three kills—before breakfast.

There was a glamour to these men and as one of them, Group Captain Tom Gleave, says today: "By and large all of them, when they arrived in their frontline squadrons, thirsted for action . . ."

Gleave, who was shot down in flames and badly burned, says: "Perhaps some of them did regard it as a game of cricket. That kind of enthusiasm helped."

But five out of twelve of these Battle of Britain pilots were to be killed before the war ended.

Sailor Malan, a South African, was one of "the greats" whom other aces still talk of, long after his death, with admiration. He became a station commander and his quotations are legendary; words which young, apprentice pilots held dear to their hearts. One of them: "Never follow a Hun down after you've hit him hard; if you're satisfied he's done for, look for another. You may find him on your tail."

The ten commandments on page 40 are Malan's; they were pinned on the mess-hut of every R.A.F. fighter station.

The ever-hungry New Zealander Al Deere, himself no mean fighter, said Malan was the most outstanding fighter pilot of the war. Winston Churchill was a great admirer of his—and became godfather to Malan's son.

The names resound like drums. Men such as John Cunningham, known as "Cat's Eyes" Cunningham because of his ability to fight in the night . . . and, of course, Robert Stanford Tuck.

He was known as "The Immortal" or "Lucky" Tuck and his shooting down of German planes was as remarkable as his skill at throwing knives—a skill he learned when in the merchant navy before the war.

He, too, was an individualist—once leading a formation of only eight planes against 50 Germans, and bringing down ten.

It is not really strange that, after the war, he met Adolf Galland and the two are now firm friends. They have, says Tuck, got hunting in common.

Such courage! But how many Victoria Crosses?

One—the only V.C. of the Battle of Britain to be won by the Royal

TEN of MY RULES for AIR FIGHTING

1 <u>Wait until you see the whites of his eyes.</u>
Fire short bursts of 1 to 2 seconds and only when your sights are definitely 'ON'.

2 Whilst shooting think of nothing else; brace the whole of the body; have both hands on the stick; concentrate on your ring sight.

3 Always keep a sharp lookout. "Keep your finger out"!

4 Height gives <u>You</u> the initiative.

5 Always turn and face the attack.

6 Make your decisions promptly. It is better to act quickly even though your tactics are not the best.

7 Never fly straight and level for more than 30 seconds in the combat area.

8 When diving to attack always leave a proportion of your formation above to act as top guard.

9 INITIATIVE, AGGRESSION, AIR DISCIPLINE, and TEAM WORK are words that MEAN something in Air Fighting.

10 Go in quickly – Punch hard – Get out!

Air Force. This was won by Flight Lieutenant James Brindley Nicholson who was hit by cannon shells, burned and wounded, and with his Hurricane cockpit blazing like a furnace chased an enemy plane, following it down until he saw it crash.

Then he tried to get out of the cockpit. But his hands had been seared by flame and it took a lot of pain before he managed to throw himself out of the plane and somersault earthwards.

He floated over Hampshire at the end of his parachute. Below him were the Home Guard—those volunteer civilians mobilised for Britain's land defences. They thought he was a German parachutist, and shot him in the bottom.

Seven Americans took part in the Battle on the side of Britain, even though their country was neutral. And there were many other names I have not the space to record here besides the Poles, the Czechs, the Canadians, the Australians, the New Zealanders, the South Africans, the French.

There was an attitude built up among the British pilots of casual humour. A crash was a "prang". If a comrade died someone might say: "He shouldn't have joined if he couldn't take a joke."

The casualness concealed a deep concern. But that was how it had to be; otherwise, as one pilot put it, "you'd have wept into your beer all night."

Because, of course, it was not a job that was performed lightly. It *was* killing. But you had to take it lightly if you were to survive.

Air Marshal Sir William Elliot said of the pilot who rode the sky at speeds of 400 miles an hour:

"Returning to earth, he is so weary and nerve-racked that he

The Germans continued to pound at the airfields. The British pilots were constantly under pressure. ▼

immediately drops asleep under the shadow of his aircraft and vomits each time that he is woken by the Tannoy to renew his place in the terrible battle which was to prove as much for the survival of his country as of himself . . .

"The battle was not of the choosing of the young men who fought it, but once it was joined, they threw themselves into it with a selfless and skilful heroism which at the time drew praise from the greatest living Englishman in words which ensure that their names and deeds are immortal."

He was talking about Churchill.

Douglas Bader talks about memories:

"Two Hurricanes converging on the same Junkers 88. You cannot shout a warning because there is no common radio frequency. The Hurricanes touch, a wing breaks off and floats away like a falling leaf. One pilot bales out and lands safely to live to continue the fight another day. You are closing on a Dornier 17 when some sixth sense makes you look up to see a Spitfire diving vertically from above. As you sheer away the Spitfire hits the Dornier fair and square. It wraps itself round the fighter and they both go down on fire and seemingly quite slowly—like a ball of paper that has been set alight and thrown into the air. A stream of bullets crashes into the dashboard of your Hurricane and you nearly die of fright as you wrench it round. You see the Messerschmitt that nearly got you go past in an ever-steepening dive with the Hurricane that has killed it on its tail. As you watch, the Messerschmitt disappears into the pall of smoke from the burning oil tanks at Shell Haven on the north bank of the Thames estuary. Of such are the memories which can still stir the blood twenty-seven years later."

These pilots never seemed to probe deeply into the depth of their emotions. But here is one poem written by a Canadian pilot, Flying Officer E. R. Davey, shortly before his death.

The Way

Almighty and All-Present Power,
Short is the prayer I make to Thee:
I do not ask in battle hour
For any shield to cover me.

The vast unalterable way,
From which the stars do not depart,
May not be turned aside to stay
The bullet flying to my heart.

I ask no help to strike my foe,
I seek no petty victory here:
The enemy I hate, I know
To Thee is dear.

But this I pray, be at my side
When death is drawing through the sky;
Almighty Lord, Who also died,
Teach me the way that I should die.

A sombre ending for a chapter about heroes? Listen then to Adolf Galland on the British pilots:

"Any encounter with British fighters called for maximum effort . . . I can only express the highest admiration for the British fighter pilots who, although technically at a disadvantage, fought bravely and indefatigably.

"They undoubtedly saved their country at this crucial hour."

They *and* Dowding, who in the loneliness of his High Command decisions had to send those young men out to die. Those men whom Churchill called "Dowding's young chicks".

For there were heroes on the ground as well as in the sky.

But perhaps what singled out the aces, the heroes, was an instinct beyond the normal—a sense of being individual.

When asked why he didn't go fox-hunting Bob Stanford Tuck, who is a great shooter of stag and deer, said: "I could never go hunting with a pack."

Perhaps that is what it was all about. However many comrades you went out to fight with, in the end you fought alone.

THE MEN... & THE MACHINES

Britain was proud of her high-flyers, her heroic pilots. The pilots were privileged to wear the top button of their tunics undone and small boys everywhere followed that example, hoping that by imitation they would be mistaken for their particular idol.

One boy heard a crash from outside his house, rushed to the source of the noise and there was an R.A.F. pilot whose parachute descent had landed him in the garden's cucumber frame.

The boy went back into the house and brought out some cigarettes which he, respectfully, handed to the pilot.

"Good luck, sir," he said. "When I grow up I'm going to be an airman, too."

The comic papers of the time were full of R.A.F. heroes. "Rockfist Rogan of the R.A.F." was one of them, although he seemed to have more brawn than brain, and brain combined with aerial cunning was definitely needed if you were to keep yourself alive in the sky.

Meanwhile, the bombing was going on; the Germans were getting through. Although Goering was not at all as pleased with events as he might have been.

By this time he had been raised to the position of Reichmarschall, a title which Hitler bestowed upon him, possibly because there were no more medals that could be given to the fat general—he had all there were, already.

He looked rather a figure of fun, but his planning, if at times reckless, was wearing on Britain. His bombers droned through British skies and, although British fighters were keeping up their average of "kills", the German bombers were still unloading their bombs on to British airfields—and British factories.

It was very deliberate. Goering wrote: "We have reached the decisive point in the air war against England. The vital task is to turn all means at our disposal to the defeat of the enemy's air force. Our first aim must be the destruction of the enemy's fighters. If they no longer take the air we must attack them on the ground or force them into battle by directing bomber targets within range of our fighters."

The weakening of British fighter strength was of prime importance, Goering wrote next day. And looking ahead to that invasion date of September 15, it was not happening as quickly as he would have liked. There were reasons.

Listen to German ace Adolf Galland: ". . . Goering came to pay us a visit in our quarters along the English Channel. The heavy bombing attacks against Britain were in preparation. The necessary air superiority had not been acquired to the extent hoped for. The British Command was hurt, but not annihilated . . ."

Goering raged at his fighter leaders, saying they hadn't enough faith in victory. Galland tried to explain to him that the Messerschmitt 109, highly useful in combat, was less suitable for defensive missions than the Spitfire—which was much more manoeuvrable.

Goering seemed to ignore this, then he turned to Galland and his rival-friend Werner Mölders. He asked them what they needed to help claw down British Fighter Command from the skies.

"Mölders," says Galland, "asked for his squadron to be equipped with a run of Me 109's with more powerful engines. Goering agreed to this. 'And you?' asked Goering, turning towards me. I did not think long. 'I request that my command be equipped with Spitfires.'

"After having said this I shivered . . . Goering went away grumbling and stamping his feet down. I did not receive any Spitfires."

It says something for the Spitfire that it was regarded with awe and longing by the enemy it pursued down the skies of Britain. But all

German pilots receive a briefing before a mission. ▼

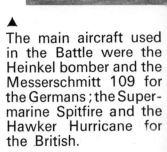

the planes that took part in the Battle of Britain took on a halo of fascination for the public for whom they were fighting.

There were four main aircraft used during the Battle. For the Germans the Heinkel bomber and its "cover" plane, the single-engine Messerschmitt 109. For the British the Supermarine Spitfire and the Hawker Hurricane.

The Heinkel 111 was the standard level bomber of the Luftwaffe. Twin-engined it could carry a bomb load of 5,510 pounds but suffered —as did all German twin-engined bombers—from the distance to targets in the North of England because it could not be guarded by its own fighter planes which had smaller fuel tanks.

Goering believed that the use of the Heinkel in mass would be a deciding factor in bringing Britain to her knees. He misjudged then . . . as he misjudged later.

The Messerschmitt 109 had a top speed of 354 m.p.h. and was known to the German pilots who flew it as "Emil". Nobody quite knows why and it's a strange name to find attached to a plane because aircraft, like ships, are usually female.

As aggressive as a terrier, this slender little plane was almost never built, because of a long-standing feud between the German Secretary of State for Air, General Erhard Milch, and its designer, Willy Messerschmitt.

The main aircraft used in the Battle were the Heinkel bomber and the Messerschmitt 109 for the Germans; the Supermarine Spitfire and the Hawker Hurricane for the British.

48

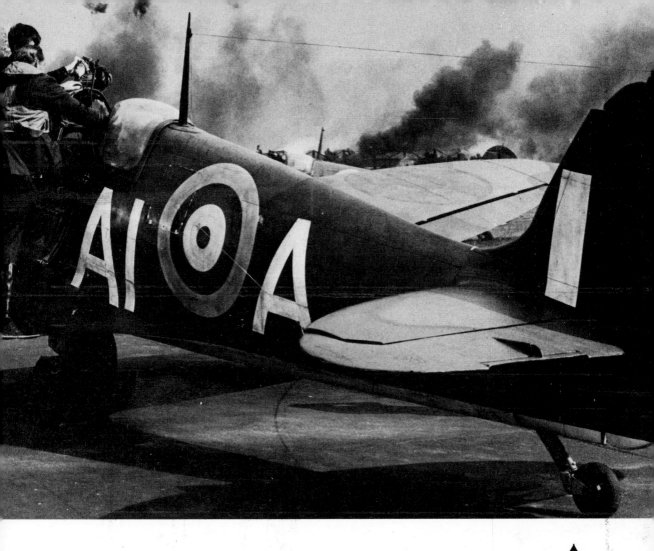

▲

British pilot entering Spitfire to defend airfield against attack.

It had disadvantages—poor vision from the cockpit; its performance was much restricted when later it was pressed into service as a fighter-bomber—but it held its own against the Hurricanes in France.

The Messerschmitt acquired a mystique—so did the Hurricane. Although the Spitfire is almost synonymous with the Battle of Britain, in fact, there were actually far more Hurricanes than Spitfires used in the Battle. At the start of the Battle there were 325 Hurricanes to 230 Spitfires ready to fight.

The pilots who flew the Hurricane knew that she was aptly named—that she could blow up a terrifying storm for the enemy. They called her the "Hurri-bus" . . . a term of affection. Paul Gallico wrote: "She was loved and trusted by every man who knew her. She was unique in the heavens . . . To her friends she was gentle, staunch, loyal and a protectress; to her enemies she was a lightning bolt from the skies, a ruthless and total destroyer. An inanimate piece of machinery, a mass of tubes, wire, steel, aluminium, she flew like an angel."

A bit over-emphatic, maybe. Ginger Lacey, who flew only Hurricanes during the Battle, said that at one time or another he had every possible part of a Hurricane blown off—and still was able to bring it in to land.

She was a fighter plane that nearly never took to the air. Designed

49

by Sydney Camm for the Hawker Aircraft Company in 1933, the Air Ministry thought that the idea of building a fighter monoplane was "cranky".

Hawker went ahead anyway. It took four thousand separate blue prints to achieve the solid perfection that the Air Ministry was later to be so proud of during the Battle of Britain.

It took flying skill, though, and for the first time in history flyers experienced blackouts if they pulled out of a dive too sharply. Its top speed was 325 miles an hour.

Fighter ace Bob Stanford Tuck had been a Spitfire pilot, but in 1940 was given command of a squadron flying Hurricanes. "My reaction to my first flight in the Hurricane after the Spits was not good. She seemed like a flying brick, a great lumbering stallion. It nearly broke my heart because things seemed tough enough without trying to tackle Messerschmitts in a great heavy kite like this.

"But after the first few minutes I found the Hurricane's virtues. She was solid and it was obvious she'd take a devil of a lot of punishment. She was steady as a rock and was a wonderful gun plat-form (she was armed with eight 0.303 inch machine guns). The visibility was far better than in the Spit. The undercart was stronger and wider and that made landing a lot easier. Somehow she gave the pilot terrific confidence. You felt entirely safe in this plane."

Sydney Camm kept working on the Hurricane. Throughout the Battle of Britain one of his test pilots, Dickie Reynell, flew service Hurricanes with different squadrons against the enemy—to see how the Hurricane worked in combat conditions. He was shot down and killed on September 9; his last report was never handed in.

The famous shape of the Spitfire grew from the Supermarine Sea Lion seaplane, winner of the Schneider Trophy Air Race in 1922. Its design and performance came from the genius of Reginald J. Mitchell, designer of every British Schneider Trophy winner since the 1914–18 war.

Mitchell died in 1937, his work being taken over until the Spitfire became the deadly bullet that it was in the Battle of Britain.

It had its faults. Its engine would cut out when it went into a dive and then pick up again, unlike the Messerschmitt whose engine was constantly working.

Its retractable undercarriage, giving it that elegant, deadly shape in the air, could be a nuisance on landing because many pilots forgot to lower that undercarriage. So a klaxon horn was fitted which blared out when speed was reduced for coming down. A kind of aerial alarm clock!

The Spitfire had the same engine as the Hurricane—the Rolls-Royce Merlin—and was the smallest and neatest fighter that could be arranged around engine, pilot and eight guns ready to spit fire. It was a plane that was marvellous to use in aerobatic displays.

Richard Hillary wrote of its "clear-cut beauty, the wicked simplicity" of its lines.

When the Battle of Britain started there were 19 Spitfire squadrons. Probably not enough—and it was certainly not a plane to be wrecked deliberately: the enemy was doing enough of that. One sergeant pilot did though. He'd been piloting as a target aircraft for camera-gun practice when his engine suddenly cut out. All he could hear was the ominous whistling of the wind. Then, below—he was over Suffolk—he saw an open field which looked good enough for a successful belly-landing.

He glided down and then saw children playing. Desperately he flew further on into the next field, where he made a crash-landing which damaged the plane, but not him!

A few of the Spitfires were armed with cannons which fired explosive shells, but these weren't popular with pilots—because so often there were stoppages and they couldn't get the kill that they had sighted.

There were other German planes, of course, the Junkers 87 (the Stuka) and 88, Dorniers 17 and 215 and Messerschmitt 110. This last was nicknamed "Goering's folly" and, although it was intended to provide long-range escort for the bombers, had to have an escort itself —so clumsy was it in the air.

But the five I have mentioned, together with the Heinkel bomber, were the aerial middleweights and heavyweights, ready to punch the R.A.F. on the ground with their bombed-up fists.

At that time—around the middle of August—it looked as though the R.A.F. was just keeping its head above the waters of surrender. But only just.

The Luftwaffe wasn't getting the rapid results that Goering wanted. His fighter pilots were annoyed because they were told they had to stick closer to the bombers; this was rather like putting a hunting-dog on a leash.

Galland reported that the short range of the Messerschmitt 109 was becoming a disadvantage. "During a single sortie of my wing we lost twelve fighter planes, not by enemy action but simply because, after two hours' flying time, the bombers we were escorting had not yet reached the mainland on their return journey.

"Five of these fighters managed to make a pancake landing on the French shore with their last drop of fuel, seven of them landing in the 'drink'."

These restrictions might annoy, but the R.A.F. *was* being eroded. It was, as we have said earlier, a question of manpower. The few pilots there were, who were properly trained, were given no respite, no rest.

Lord Dowding talked about the miracle that was needed to save them, because he realised what would happen to the R.A.F.—and the country—if things went on as they were going.

Retreat, as one writer put it, was in the air. On August 24 the fighter bases at Kenley, Croydon, Biggin Hill, West Malling, Hornchurch, Rochford, North Weald, Debden, Hawkinge, Lympne and Manston— a protective ring around London—seemed almost to be on the point of collapse, so intensive was the bombing to which they had been subjected.

Manston airfield was completely abandoned.

The morale of the pilots was high, but those in command knew it was a false optimism.

A miracle? It came. It made thousands homeless, killed thousands, shocked civilians into the front line along with the pilots. But it was a kind of miracle; a brutal miracle.

BLITZ

We don't know his name. He was a pilot in a German Heinkel bomber on that day of August 24. But we can imagine the scene within the cramped confines of the bomber, stinking of oil and fumes and metal. He and his navigator were probably tired and harassed. It had been an exhausting run . . .

Would the British never give in? Couldn't they see that there was no hope? How could there be? Hitler's Germany would last, if not for ever, nearly as long. Those impossible British! Why, a German pilot had dropped pamphlets on their towns telling them of Hitler's "appeal to reason". And what had they done? Held auctions for the pamphlets to raise money for charities. Really, they were impossible!

Whereabouts, over this country, were they now? A radio beam from Europe had been a useful marker for the German bombers, helping them to pinpoint targets, but the British had cottoned on to that and interfered with it so that, often, Germans went off course.

Had that happened now? The navigator was bewildered. The fuel gauge looked dangerously low, especially if they were to get back over the English Channel. That was really the frightening thing; not the anti-aircraft fire, not even the fighters . . . you expected those and you fought like a man. But crashing in water was something to be afraid of. Death by drowning . . . !

The best thing to do was to drop the bombs anywhere. Here was as good a place as any.

And so an unknown pilot pressed the button that was to lay those deadly "eggs" and to start Phase Three of the Battle of Britain, and to become Nazi Germany's biggest blunder.

Until now no deliberate bombs had been dropped on civilians. The terrible weapon of the blitz—sharpened and bloodied in Europe—had been sheathed. Bombers on both sides went for military targets.

Of course civilians were killed if a bomb landed off-target (and there's really not much difference between an accidental death and a deliberate one!), but on the whole both sides had scruples about attacking defenceless civilians. Or seemed to have.

And then those bombs dropped accidentally on the heart of London and smashed all ideas of chivalry into a million forgotten fragments.

Churchill hit back at Berlin. It was a reprisal raid of 81 British bombers and they hit fair and square at Germany's capital city. It

"And then those bombs
dropped accidentally on
the heart of London—"

▲
The bombs continued
to fall on South East
England, destroying
thousands of civilian
homes.

also hit hard at Goering's pride, because he had said that no enemy bomb would ever fall on Berlin. Now the debris-strewn streets, and shattered houses, showed that he had been a fool to make such a vain boast.

It took time for the fact to sink in, but when it did it left a shaming wound.

For the moment the attacks went on in South East England, battering the airfields with no respite. Waves of two or three hundred bombers would come over, each moving away to their selected target-airfields.

Biggin Hill was badly mauled on September 1. Operations rooms everywhere were demolished, airfields were unusable because they were cratered with bomb-blasts.

Wearing their tin hats the girls of the Women's Auxiliary Air Force found themselves as much in the front line as those pilots who flew up to fight for their lives. Keeping in telephone touch with other airfields the girls would often, courageously, carry on working even though the bombers were right overhead.

Some of them won medals to give visible evidence of their bravery. All had courage of the highest order. It was needed now as the bombing attacks by the Germans mounted towards a screaming peak of destruction.

Hornchurch fighter-ace Al Deere said: "My section was nearly airborne when the first bomb fell. The next second, a one thousand pounder dropped plumb in front of my nose . . . I seemed to be flung miles into the air, then my machine flicked on to its back and crashed on to the aerodrome to career upside down for some 250 yards. My head was scraped along the ground and slowly but surely I was being squeezed into a ball in the cockpit.

"At last the aircraft stopped. Everything was pitch black. The earth shook with the explosion of bombs. My mouth was full of blood and grit; my head rested in a pool of petrol from the burst tank.

"It was frightening, balancing there on my head, realising that with one spark I would be enveloped in flaming petrol. Then a voice called out: 'Are you all right, Al?' Spitting out mouthfuls of earth I bawled, 'Yes, but for hell's sake get me out of here.' "

It was agreed that this was the worst time yet for British Fighter Command. The Luftwaffe Eagle had its claws sunk deep into the neck of its opponent. It was not going to let go.

On the other side of the Channel, as if sensing victory, preparations for invasion mounted like a tidal wave. In Britain rumours were rife that the invasion *had* started, that German troops had been seen, but that wasn't true . . . yet.

However, in Europe nearly a quarter of a million troops began to take up positions along the coast. There were between 30,000 and 40,000 vehicles including "amphibians". There were nearly 65,000 horses and 500 field howitzers and more than fifty anti-aircraft batteries and rocket projectors besides a mass of landing gear.

A great armada of barges, tugs and motor-boats was assembled. Not even nightly raids by British Bomber Command could rattle the steady growth of these forces.

We know now what the plans were: three operations in all, including

Victims of the blitz, their homes destroyed, gather for safety in a church hall in East London.

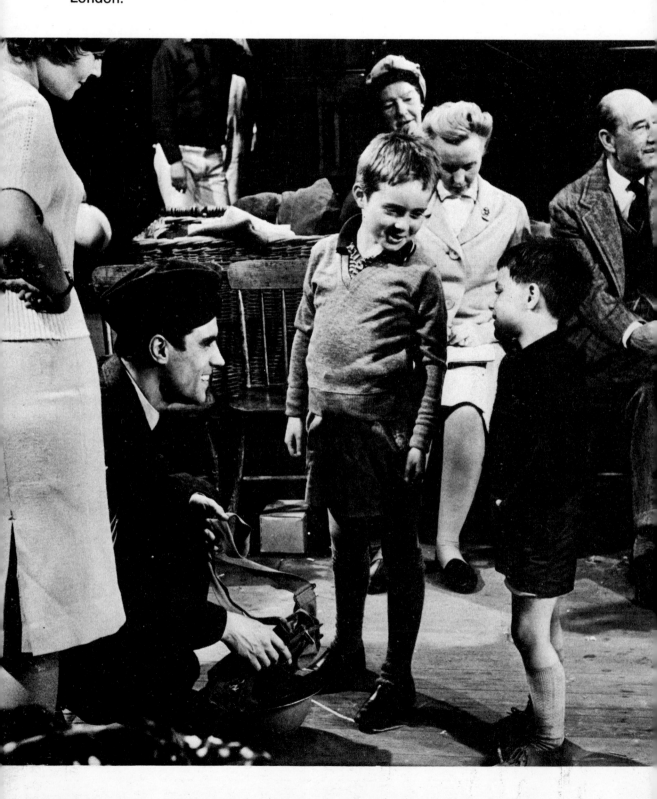

attacks on Beachy Head and Brighton; Camber and Eastbourne; and Folkestone and New Romney. Field Marshal von Brauchitsch issued this order:

"After the arrival of sufficient forces on British soil the Army Group will attack and secure possession of the line [north of the] Thames Estuary—heights south of London-Portsmouth. As soon as the situation permits, mobile formations will be pushed forward to the area west of London in order to cut off London from the south and west and to capture crossings over the Thames for an advance in the direction of Watford-Swindon."

There were even plans to deport able-bodied men and a Black List was drawn up of "Enemies of The Reich". Top of the list, of course, was Winston Churchill.

Invasion had never seemed so frighteningly near.

If it had happened, if Britain had been over-run, the world would be a completely different place today. And it nearly happened.

But then the wound of the Berlin-bombing began to hurt. And on September 4 Hitler stepped out on to the rostrum at the mighty hall of the Sportspalast in Berlin to make a speech—and the biggest mistake of his life.

He had been told that British Fighter Command was now so weak that it was tottering. He did not believe it when others assured him this was not the case. *He* knew better.

And he told the hysterically-devoted women at that Sportspalast: "I have waited three months without responding, with the thought that they might stop this mischief. Herr Churchill saw in this a sign of weakness. When they declare that they will attack our cities in great strength, then we will eradicate their cities.

"Last night bombs were dropped on Berlin. So be it. Two can play at that game. If the R.A.F. drops 200, 300 or 400 bombs, then in one night we will drop 2,000, 3,000 4,000 bombs! If they attack our cities then we will wipe theirs out! The hour will come when one of us must crack and it will never be National Socialist Germany. Never! Never! The English are filled with curiosity. They keep asking 'Why doesn't he come?' Be patient. We are coming. We are coming!"

His listeners cheered until they were hoarse. Hitler would show them. He was their Fuehrer! Their leader!

On September 7 the blitz started on London, all day and all night. An average of 200 bombers nightly swooped upon the city.

And the bombing on South-East airfields practically stopped. Thus giving Dowding and his men a chance to regain their strength. The airfields desperately needed a rest from the bombing—a chance for wounds to heal; to gather their self-confidence and their pilots for the future. In London darkness and death fell from the air.

▶

In the aftermath of a German raid a young boy stands alone in the ruins of a church.

THE CIVILIAN AS HERO

Whistle while you work,
Old Hitler is a squirt.
Goering's barmy—
So's his army.
Rub them in the dirt!

(To be sung to the "Whistle
While You Work" tune from Walt
Disney's film *Snow White And
The Seven Dwarfs*.)

The blitz on London began on September 7 and brought the aerial combat down to earth—to give the civilians of Britain hero-status alongside the fighter-pilots.

On that day Reichmarschall Goering, as though unable to contain his enthusiasm for the event, arrived at the Pas de Calais in France and from the cliffs at Cap Gris-Nez looked across those 22 miles of English Channel. Overhead three hundred bombers and six hundred fighters massed for the blitz upon London . . . for the capital city was what Hitler *really* meant when he talked about "eradicating their cities".

He figured that if London were knocked out the fighting breath of Britain would gasp out like a pricked balloon.

London, of course, was a military target as well as a civil one. There were many factories there, it was Britain's biggest port—and the political and military leaders lived there. And thousands of civilians . . . men, women and children . . . were suddenly thrust into the front line of the war.

In a way British Fighter Command was caught off guard by Hitler's sudden switch to blitz-tactics. There had been an attack on Hawkinge airfield that morning; it thought that the next assault would again, wearyingly, be on another airfield. It was common-sense, after all, to continue bashing away at your enemy's weakest point—and the airfields were definitely Britain's weakest point at that moment.

Radar spotted it first—the build-up of planes over the French coast. Then the troops on the coast saw the massive swarming of those deadly bees heading for the hive of London.

This attack was going to be different. In two huge waves, in un-broken formation, the bombers and their escorts headed northwards

towards London. One formation turned eastwards towards the dock-yards of Tilbury and the Thameshaven oil tanks. The second made directly for London.

Whole districts in the capital's East End sprouted fire, scores of people were killed or crippled . . . the smoke from burning oil tanks billowed upwards like a funeral pall for a dying city.

Ed Murrow, the American commentator, said: ". . . the bombers came at dusk and left at dawn and the Germans were expected on the beaches the first foggy morning . . . It was like a shuttle service the way the German planes came up the Thames, the fires acting as a flare path. Often they were above the smoke. The searchlights bored into that black roof but couldn't penetrate it. They looked like long pillars supporting a black canopy. The shrapnel clicked on the road and still the German bombers came."

To those on Britain's side the day and night of September 7 were a dismal spectacle. There was the distant clang-clang as an under-staffed Fire Brigade with volunteers raced to more and more fires, and air-raid wardens calling to people to "take cover" in the underground shelters. The city burned red.

On the night of September 7 three main-line terminal railway stations were put out of action. Four hundred and thirty men, women and children had been killed; 1,600 seriously wounded.

The further facts are that from September 7 until the end of the month London was bombed every night. Killed: 5,730 people. Badly injured: 10,000.

These were terrifying figures, eased only by the fact that on September 7 some of the Dornier bombers, still gloating over their meal of destruction, were caught by the 303 (Polish) Squadron who fell upon them as the Germans turned homewards. The Poles had a debt to repay with vengeance for the surrender of their homeland!

But even that could not prevent the feeling of great loss. One Polish pilot wrote: "I turned back from this chase but I was returning with a heavy heart, in spite of my victories, for the whole eastern suburb of London seemed to be burning. It was a very sorrowful sight, reminding me of a flight a year ago over Poland, near Lublin; it was the same spectacle."

And Goering, confident now, seemed to hammer home the message when he told the German people: "This is the historic hour when our air force for the first time delivered its stroke right into the enemy's heart."

But what did that heart do? It beat faster. It beat harder.

What do you do when the worst that can happen—happens? It depends on the kind of person you are. What happened when London came under siege was that the British spirit stiffened into a kind of passive defiance.

Death was all around as the blitz mounted in the days following September 7, so Londoners laughed about it. There wasn't much else they could do. They made up daft songs about the enemy who was bullying them with such bloody regularity every night. Stories and jokes grew as rapidly as the London Pride weed—about which Noel Coward wrote a song—which enveloped the bombed sites.

There was one woman who took her little girl into the air raid

61

shelter and sang her a lullaby. Said the girl: "Do you mind not singing, Mummy? I want to hear the bombs go off."

There was the housemaid at the hotel who knocked on the visitor's door and said, calmly, as the sirens screamed and the thump-thump of bombs began: "Bombs, please, sir!"

And the old gentleman of seventy who refused to go down into the air raid shelter because "I have to keep my canary company as he gets nervous at the noise."

Flying ace Peter Townsend said: "It must have been awful. At least, if you were a fighter pilot, you could fight back. But if you were a civilian you couldn't do anything but grin and bear it."

That was one of the slogans of the time: "Grin And Bear It". And, as each blitz morning revealed the extent of the damage done by at least two hundred German bombers the night before, signs went up on shop windows proclaiming: "Business As Usual".

It seemed impossible that there could be "business as usual".

As one observer wrote at that time, watching from across the Thames from Lambeth: ". . . the whole of London seemed involved, one great circle of overwhelming disaster save in one corner where the night sky was clear. One could not distinguish known buildings through the great clouds of smoke, except when there was a sudden spurt of yellow flames which lit a church tower. It seemed impossible that the city, that London, could be saved."

But what had happened in the skies was happening on the ground. The peculiar spirit of unity that had drawn together British fighter pilots into a dynamic fighting unit clenched Londoners into a fist of defiance.

People looking back on that time talk about how comradely you felt towards your neighbour. There was talk of looting, but Lady Rose Henriques, an organiser for blitz relief, who lived in Stepney—two thirds of which was bombed flat in the 1940 blitz—said: "I never saw any signs of looting. Anything that was visible was completely sacred.

"I saw the utmost generosity towards those who had lost their homes. I never found anybody saying 'Why did this happen to me?'

"Morale was much higher than in the first war . . . magnificent fellowship . . . the papers gave the score rather like a cricket score."

On the radio the B.B.C. announcers calmly told the news as it happened. It is said that the German bomber-pilots, over London, were astonished to tune in to British wavebands. Because they heard dance bands playing the songs of the moment and, on one channel, a speaker describing how he kept racing pigeons. The mad British!

There was another radio voice, much liked by the British, although what he said was supposed to bring fear into their hearts. This was the voice of William Joyce, nicknamed Lord Haw-Haw by the irreverent Cockneys.

His German-propaganda broadcasts, detailing exaggerated accounts of death and destruction, brought roars of laughter in the packed underground shelters and his snooty way of opening his programme—"Jairmany Calling, Jairmany Calling"—was a ripe joke for the weary Londoners.

Of course, the blitz was to extend beyond London to other cities. Coventry, Southampton, Bristol, Cardiff, Sheffield and Liverpool . . .

A lone Heinkel bomber
flying over South East
England; its mission—
destruction . . .

just a few of the chopping-blocks to fall under the axe of the Luftwaffe. But for those days of September it was London that was the main victim of the assault.

Every house had a hero, every street a joke. One woman remembers how, after her house had been bombed for the third time, she had to rig up a bathroom with blankets hung up as walls.

"Just as I took my clothes off the bombs started dropping again. And I had to run to the shelter, clutching my clothes to me as best I could."

The bombs were usually a mixture of high-explosives and incendiaries (which explode and spray-burn a large area); and units of air raid wardens dashed here and there, armed only with stirrup pumps and sand to put out such incendiaries.

One team worked through the night to rescue a woman who had been trapped under a heap of bricks, mortar and wooden beams. They were joined by a fighter pilot Richard Hillary, who had been badly scarred during one sky-combat.

For Hillary it was an emotional night. The woman's child had been killed. Then the woman saw that Hillary had been one of her rescuers. Immediately her sympathy went out to him, as she saw his burned face. She held his hand. "I see they got you, too," she said.

Although the East End, being so near to the docks, bore the biggest brunt of the bombing, bombs did drop on Buckingham Palace and this, strangely, had an uplifting effect on the Cockneys.

Said one of them: "You realised that the King and Queen were in there with you, there was no class distinction; they were under fire as well. The fact that they stayed in London when they could have so easily shifted their headquarters further North was a great boost to all of us."

Londoners needed that boost. In their streets they saw debris and death. Even if the bombers didn't knock things down, the Government did. Lord Beaverbrook, pressing ahead strongly to produce fighter planes, had all the railings from public parks removed—and his slogan "A saucepan for a Spitfire" meant that you just *had* to hand over all your old ironware to turn it into fighting power for the country . . .

But what were the fighters doing? For all practical purposes they were unable to operate at strength during the night and the Germans' main assaults came during darkness.

Although some attacks came during the day, and these were vigorously turned by the British, London seemed at times defenceless —armed only by the ring of anti-aircraft guns. It's been estimated that in 68 nights more than 13,000 tons of high explosives and more than 12,000 canisters of incendiary bombs were dropped—enough to burn away the spirit of a whole nation.

But what was happening to Operation Sealion—Hitler's proposed invasion of Britain? The Fuehrer was still not convinced that he should set in motion the machinery that would start the Operation on September 15. He delayed.

On September 10 a daylight raid by bombers was shattered by British fighters, but next day Churchill sounded a warning for all. Invasion seemed to be almost at hand.

He said: "Several hundreds of self-propelled barges are moving

▶ September 10, a daylight raid by German bombers was shattered by British fighters but invasion still seemed near at hand . . .

down the coasts of Europe . . . convoys of merchant ships in tens and dozens are being moved through the Straits of Dover into the Channel . . .

"If this invasion is to be tried at all it does not seem it can be long delayed. Therefore we must regard the next week or so as a very important period in our history.

"It ranks with the days when the Spanish Armada was approaching the Channel. . . or when Nelson stood between us and Napoleon's Grand Army at Boulogne."

The day of reckoning was looming. September 15 was at hand. The day promised by Hitler to his impatient Generals.

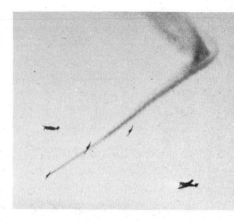

But there *had* been a respite. The blitz had been a miracle. Said Air Vice Marshal Park, whose No. 11 Group had suffered the worst of the early stages of the Battle of Britain: "On the late evening of September 7 I flew over London on my way back from visiting my battered fighter aerodromes, and I can assure you that the East End of London and the Thames Estuary were a grim sight as a result of the many fires that were burning.

"However, though I felt very angry, I said 'Thank God', because I realised that the methodical Germans had at last switched their attacks from my vital aerodromes on to cities. I felt confident that we could win as long as I could continue to operate the fighter squadrons."

It was a realistic look at what was happening, a happening that brought the civilians under the shock of blitz. "I see they got you too," the pilot could have said to the woman . . .

Eight days after September 7 the civilians knew that their sacrifice had not been in vain. Something big was about to break. Could it be the German Luftwaffe?

BLITZ!
BLITZ!

DAY OF RECKONING

History is what you live through. But there are never any little flags set up to mark the fact that what you are witnessing is a historic occasion. *That* you have to sort out later on—when you've got all the facts and the answers come out of what those facts tell you.

So it was with September 15, the day now regarded as Battle of Britain Day. It can now be seen as one of those times when the pendulum-might of the German offensive reached the top of its swing and started to fall.

But how many really knew that at the time? Every year members of the Battle of Britain Fighter Association gather at the Bentley Priory Headquarters at Stanmore and, there, look back on September 15, 1940, as perhaps one of the most illustrious in the history of the Royal Air Force.

I asked several members of the Association if they knew it was such a great day at the time? None of them did. They were too close to the exercise; unable to separate the wood from the trees until later.

Because, as you'll have gathered, the Battle of Britain was unlike most other battles that have been fought. Usually, battles have a final ending, a grand hurrah when you know who has won.

But the Battle of Britain has been likened to a boxing match, in which there was no knock-out blow. It was just that one boxer failed to get back into the ring. And the referee of history held up the hand of the R.A.F.—to proclaim it the winner.

This we know now. But try to think yourself back to that time and wonder just how worried and scared you might have been. The smell of invasion was everywhere. Even Winston Churchill had spoken about it on the night of September 11.

And that was the twenty-four hours when the Luftwaffe lost only 25 aircraft—four fewer than the R.A.F. A bleak prospect. It was September 15 that was to turn the tide a fraction, so that it could be afterwards called "the most decisive day of the Battle of Britain", because of its effect on Hitler and his men.

On September 14 Hitler had called off Operation Sealion, an animal whose bark was worse than its bite, for three days. The order read:

> (a) The start of the operation is again postponed. A new order follows on September 17. All preparations are to be continued.

(b) As soon as preparations are complete, the Luftwaffe is to carry out attacks against the British long-range batteries.

(c) The measures planned for the evacuation of the coastal area are not to be set in motion to the full extent. Counter-espionage and deception measures are, however, to be increased.

British pilots watch the return of a lone Spitfire after a raid.

Hitler wanted the moon and tide to be just right for the invasion. Despite Intelligence reports he felt that the R.A.F. had not been completely knocked out of the skies—and he had to have complete control of the air. Goering decided to mount a major air offensive on September 15; an attack that would prove to the Fuehrer that it was safe to continue Operation Sealion.

Looking back it was a strange timidity on the part of Hitler. Almost as though he couldn't afford failure in the eyes of the rest of the world . . .

September 15 was a Sunday. Another of those bright, sunny mornings that fighter pilots hated so much because there was little or no cloud-cover in which to dodge—and from which to spring.

Winston Churchill visited No. 11 Group's headquarters at Uxbridge that morning to see what was going on. His visits to airfields, usually accompanied by Mrs. Churchill, gave him a keen insight into how the battle was being fought. His defiant victory-sign and bull-dog presence, wherever he went, raised the temperature of the morale.

It's reported that as the Prime Minister sat down to watch the W.A.A.F. plotters moving their counters in the operations room—each counter showing an aerial move of either friend or foe—Air Vice Marshal Park

BLITZ!
BLITZ!

An Operations Room, where the positions of enemy aircraft (left) were tracked.
◀

said: "I don't know whether anything will happen today. At present all is quiet."

With such a dramatic audience as Churchill, it obviously couldn't stay that way for long. It didn't. At eleven-thirty the first German aircraft crossed the south coast. Radar had once more helped: it had told of large formations massing on the European coastline.

Quietly and efficiently the girls moved the counters around the enormous board. Orders went, via telephone, to pilots and anti-aircraft gunners.

Out of Park's twenty-one squadrons in his Group eleven were up in the air in pairs of like planes—Spitfires paired with Spitfires. Besides those squadrons a squadron came zooming in from No. 10 Group.

The first actions took place above Canterbury. Heinkels, Junkers and Dorniers moved ominously onwards towards London, and among the first bombs to fall upon London, one—it failed to explode—fell within the grounds of Buckingham Palace.

But so harried were the bombers that they had to loose their bombs as best they could—often on targets too far afield to hurt anyone. But they came in their hundreds, moving from 15,000 feet up to 22,000 feet, protected by fighters.

But, besides No. 11 Group's squadrons, there now emerged from further up the map of Britain a five-squadron formation from No. 12 Group, which was to help hit a devastating blow at the Germans.

There had been arguments about tactics in Fighter Command. Air Vice Marshal Park wanted his No. 11 Group airfields given better protection—and he expected No. 12 Group planes to help do that.

But Air Vice Marshal Leigh-Mallory, at No. 12 Group, wanted to win the aerial war. He didn't want to send up his fighters in small numbers. He and Squadron Leader Douglas Bader believed in the "Big Wing"—a giant massing of fighters that could take on the Germans on equal terms.

But any arguments were forgotten on this day of days. Now No. 12 Group was as much involved as No. 11. And the Germans just hadn't reckoned that there were that many fighters to contend with. It was as though an old lady about to be attacked by a thug had drawn a machine gun out of her handbag . . .

The bombers just could not reach their targets. A flaming sword of fighter-planes stood between them and their planned destination.

The whole of the South East was caught under a web of criss-crossing vapour trails.

In London you could hear the scream of dying aircraft, the distant thunder of anti-aircraft guns and you might not be blamed if you thought the Germans had landed.

Some Germans had landed—but only because their Dorniers and Heinkels had been shot down. They came down on Kennington Oval Cricket Ground and were shot down by Sergeant R. T. Holmes of 504 Hurricane Squadron based at Hendon. His story is a mixture of comedy and terror:

"We went through cumulus cloud at eight thousand feet. This was quite dicey, for we had only practised formation flying in cloud in pairs, and to suddenly find twelve of us climbing through this bumpy stuff was quite a rare experience. Before we reached twelve thousand feet over base we'd been vectored off to rendezvous with another Hurricane squadron from North Weald at seventeen thousand feet, but we met the Dorniers first and we went straight in on a starboard quarter attack.

"I personally think far too little has been said about the part our radar played in winning the Battle of Britain. We were given a perfect interception of these Dorniers at exactly their height, which must have shaken the Hun no end and made him wonder just how many squadrons we had on patrol. Without our ground control, interceptions would have been very few and far between, and the Hun would have been through time and again.

"By then the Dornier formation had become ragged, and was turning for home, and 504 had broken away to reform and I spotted three Dorniers blazing a lone trail towards London. No one seemed to have noticed them, so I decided to give them a little attention. I made quarter attacks separately on the two outside men first, attacking from the flank and breaking away to come up on the other flank. The first man belched oil all over my windscreen, blotting my vision entirely; but when the oil cleared, due to my overtaking speed, I saw his tail very close to my nose, and one of his airscrews stopped, and just grazed under his belly as I went past below him.

"It was the second plane which caught fire at his wing root and from which came a parachutist who draped himself so artistically over my

N THE AIR

wing. I didn't give much for the chances of either of these machines getting home, but could not claim them destroyed as I had not seen them crash. I was officially credited with two probables for them.

"The leader still pressed on. One stern attack, without much apparent effect, left me low in ammo, for we only had a total of fifteen seconds' firing. I thought a head-on attack might cool his ardour, and climbed up and past him to his left for my last breakaway. It was then my engine sounded rough and I saw my oil pressure had dropped and there was oil bubbling up the inside of my windscreen—my own oil. I made the head-on attack but during it actually ran out of ammo. I knew the engine had had it anyway, so, more in frustration than in hate, I kept on and clipped one side of his fragile-looking twin tail with my port wing.

"There was only a slight bump, and I thought his tail had snapped off without harming my wing, but my port wing started slowly to dip, and the nose to drop, and I looked out and saw the end of my wing had torn away. There was no choice but to try and bale out. Sliding back the hood was fairly easy, but trying to get out into that slipstream made me feel I was putting my head in the airscrew blades themselves. At this point I entered the cloud, and knew I was half-way down already. My R.T. headphones, oxygen mask and goggles were blown off my helmet and it was quite impossible to open my eyes. I worked my feet on to the seat to push my body out, but the parachute pack caught under the hood.

"Finally my feet found the control column and I kicked that forward, and the negative G spewed me free. Unfortunately I hit the tail with my shoulder as I left the machine, so that my right arm was useless for pulling the rip-cord. Precious seconds were lost while I worked my left hand under my left armpit and pulled the ring. There was a jerk so sickening that both my boots flew off my feet, and then complete silence, and I said to myself in awe: 'It worked.'

"My vision cleared for me to see a cobweb of railway lines three hundred feet below converging on to Victoria Station, and just above the station the front half of the Dornier floating lazily like an autumn leaf on to the station roof. Ten seconds after seeing this, I hit a Cheslea roof-top myself, missed my grip, and rolled off into a dustbin.

"I slipped out of the harness into a deserted garden, and shouted: 'Is anyone at home?' Two girls popped their heads out of a next-door basement window where they had been sheltering during the air raid: so I jumped over the fence into their garden, and they came up to me and I kissed them both.

"Then I phoned my squadron. When I told the operator I was a fighter pilot who wished to contact his base at Hendon, my phone call, which would have taken anything up to two hours with delays in those days, was through in seconds. Then I had to persuade a husky Home Guard, who came rushing into the room with a length of lead piping in his hand, that I was on his side and not a German parachutist; and he proudly walked me along Ebury Bridge Road followed by a crowd of curious Londoners to some cross-roads where a fifteen foot deep crater marked the grave of my little Hurricane. I wondered how I'd have got on if we'd delayed parting company another couple of seconds.

▲

German gunner in the glass front of the Heinkel—the peace before the fight.

76

"The Home Guard also took me to Chelsea Barracks, where I asked the medical officer to check if the harness had yanked out all of my guts when the canopy caught on the down spout.

"We'd had one panic that morning before breakfast. The squadron had been put on 'thirty minutes available' and I had brekker and took my mail to read in the bath. I had been hauled out of this on to readiness, in slacks and open-necked sports shirt and flying boots with no socks, and by the time the squadron brake arrived at the dispersal, the tannoys were blaring to scramble and orbit at angels twelve.

"At Chelsea Barracks the Commanding Officer asked, looking at my bare feet, sports shirt and flannel bags, whether the R.A.F. always dressed like that. There was a call for me while I was there. A lady was asking for me from the road. I went outside, and through the railings she passed me a box of 50 Player's. 'Thank you,' she said, 'for missing our flats with your aeroplane. My baby was asleep under the stairs and she might have been killed.'

"I didn't tell her I hadn't a clue where my aeroplane was going, and I didn't tell her I didn't smoke. She could not afford those cigarettes. I was so touched I couldn't tell her anything except 'Thank you'."

Prime Minister Churchill, who had been watching all from the vantage point of that Uxbridge Operations Room, later wrote: "Hitherto I had watched in silence. I now asked 'What other reserves have we?' 'There are none,' said Air Vice Marshal Park."

Then the bombers turned tail for home. They were back again twice before the day was through—also mounting smaller attacks on Portland and Southampton.

The Germans came back in the afternoon because, if they had listened to their Intelligence services, they probably believed that the British efforts were the death agonies of a dying Air Force.

They were wrong . . . as one Dornier crew discovered. A British

Hurricane ready for action at a moment's notice.
▼

fighter pilot wrote: "Coming in to attack I noticed what appeared to be a red light shining in the rear gunner's cockpit, but when I got closer I realised I was looking right through the gunner's cockpit into the pilot and observer's cockpit beyond. The red light was fire.

"I gave it a quick burst and as I passed him on the right I looked in through the big glass nose of the Dornier. It was like a furnace inside.

"He began to go down and we watched. In a few seconds the tail came off and the bomber did a forward somersault and then went into a spin . . . The battle was over by then. I couldn't see anything else to shoot at, so I flew home."

Many pilots—so efficient was the organisation now—were able to land home, re-fuel and then take up their places again in the British fighter formations.

But true glory is not something you can wave like a flag, flutter as a banner. It also has to do with steadfastness as well as high heroism. And it was steadfastness that was needed as well as courage during that Sunday.

One pilot wrote: "Three missions today. The whole German Air Force seemed to be airborne. Action everywhere and on every mission. By the end of the day I was tired, annoyed at being shot at so frequently and feeling rather sick. I was not alone in my feelings."

The next day Winston Churchill said: "Yesterday eclipses all previous records of the Fighter Command. Aided by squadrons of their Czech and Polish comrades, using only a small proportion of their total strength and under cloud conditions of some difficulty, they cut to rags and tatters three separate waves of murderous assault upon the civil population of their native land . . . these results exceed all expectations and give just and sober confidence in the approaching struggle."

Although the figures were exaggerated by both sides on the day, the fact remains that the Germans lost 60 aircraft against only 25 for the R.A.F.

Park's paired squadrons had won the day. Britain had won the day. By replacing tired pilots with others from quieter areas, Air Chief Marshal Dowding had kept up a transfusion of courage that the massive German onslaught could not daunt.

So the day ended. Not really, though, on a note of great optimism. Air Vice Marshal Park said to Churchill at Uxbridge: "We are very glad, sir, you have seen this . . . This shows you the limitation of our present resources. They have been strained far beyond their limits today."

Now we can see that the day was a day of glory for the R.A.F. and, for the Luftwaffe, a day of reckoning. Because the mighty Eagle of the Luftwaffe was bleeding. For the first time it was shown not to be invincible.

Three years later the *Washington Star* newspaper in America wrote: "There is scarcely a doubt that historians of the future will say that September 15, 1940, was the day when Adolf Hitler's bid for world domination was doomed to ultimate failure."

The British did not know this then. They waited for the next attack —and wondered from where it would come.

BREAKDOWN

Hermann Goering was to decide that. That special train of his, in which he loved to move around Europe, steamed into Boulogne and his fieldmarshals and generals sighed. They knew they were in for another lecture from their large leader. They were.

Although it was a day of drizzle, it didn't dampen Goering's spirits. Four days of good weather and the R.A.F. could *still* be rubbed out from the skies. They were to be denied rest and relief. It could work. It *could* work . . . perhaps his optimism may have seemed a little hysterical. His reputation, as well as his Luftwaffe's, was at stake.

Others were less hysterical, more sensible in their judgement of what had happened. On the 17th, Hitler met his chiefs of High Command to decide what had to be done about that mythical beast, Operation Sealion. It was to remain a myth.

In the German Naval Staff's War Diary is recorded this entry:

"The enemy air force is still by no means defeated; on the contrary it shows increasing activity. The weather situation as a whole does not permit us to expect a period of calm. The Fuehrer has therefore decided to postpone Operation Sealion indefinitely."

The bombing went on, London being hit the hardest although now the disaster-bringing bombers were fanning out to bring cities such as Coventry within their deadly reach.

The Luftwaffe would often make a feint attack and then, when British fighters were otherwise occupied, would lunge in for a killing strike. They had now realised that daylight raids—after their experience of September 15—made them too vulnerable to British Fighter Command. September 18 was the last of the daylight raids on London when 70 bombers tried to break through and all but failed.

"London Can Take It" was the slogan of the moment. And London had to take it—from the persistent battering night-raids with which the enemy was trying to wear down the British morale. British Bomber Command hit back. At the invasion forces lined up in Europe, and on September 23—and how this cheered up Londoners—at Germany's capital, Berlin, itself.

An interesting difference in tactics shows here. Some members of the War Cabinet wanted the Berlin raid to be a terror-raid, dropping parachute mines on to targets civil and military alike. But the R.A.F. insisted that the targets be military and won the day on that issue.

Daily Mail

LATE WAR NEWS SPECIAL

FOR KING AND EMPIRE

NO. 13,852   MONDAY, SEPTEMBER 16, 1940   ONE PENNY

GREATEST DAY FOR RAF

Half Raiders Brought Down

26 FT. DOWN

350 CAME, ONLY 175 RETURNED

HITLER'S air force returned to mass daylight raids yesterday and the R.A.F. gave them the most shattering defeat they have ever known.

The Air Ministry state that between 350 and 400 enemy aircraft were launched in two waves against London and south-east England.

Of these no fewer than 175 were shot down, four of them by A.A. fire. This is a proportion of nearly one in two destroyed. All these are "certainties," for the total does not include "probables."

The R.A.F. lost 30 'planes, and ten of the pilots are safe.

Most of the raiders that were not destroyed were harassed all the way back to France.

A considerable section of Hitler's invasion fleet in the Channel ports have now been destroyed by the R.A.F.

On Saturday night our bombers gave the invasion ports their most severe battering to date.—See Back Page.

The ports of Antwerp, Ostend, Flushing, Dunkirk, Calais, and Boulogne were heavily bombed by strong forces.

Supply depots at Osnabruck, Mannheim, Aachen, Hamm, Krefeld and Brussels were attacked, and also rail communications.

Pilots and crews pressed home attacks in spite of severe weather. Gun emplacements at Cap Gris Nez and enemy aerodromes were also bombed.

DOUBLED

Reliable reports reaching Vichy, the seat of Marshal Pétain's Government, quoted by B.U.P., are that R.A.F. raids have doubled in intensity in the past 48 hours.

R.A.F. activity "is now enormously in excess of that of the Germans."

The British Fleet and Air Force are said to be keeping up a 24-hours attack on Nazi shipping at ports in Norway, Holland, Belgium, and occupied France.

The Air Ministry News Service reporting on yesterday's daylight raids, says the first wave came in the morning. At 11.30 a.m. about 200 bombers and fighters began to cross the Kentish coast.

In about eight or ten different groups they streamed in between Dover and Dungeness.

MAIN ATTACKS

The second attack came at about 2.15 p.m., when about ten groups of bombers and fighters, totalling 150 to 200 in all, crossed the same stretch of coast.

Later in the afternoon two smaller attacks were made on the Portland-Southampton areas.

In every case fighter patrols were ready to meet the enemy.

The two main attacks on the London area received such a grueling as never before. Spitfire and Hurricane squadrons, many of them veterans in London defence, fought them over the Kent coast as they came in, fought them over the Medway, and Canterbury, above the Medway, and Thames Estuary.

Many they turned back. The survivors they fought again over London itself.

Squadron after squadron of fighters flew fresh into action.

Finally they chased them back again and out over the Channel whence they came.

A squadron of Hurricanes which destroyed nine of the enemy, began the day's over London and Kent.

Another chased a group of bombers from the Thames at Hammersmith to Beachy Head, shooting down five of their number on the way.

ITALIANS 'SEVERELY HANDLED'

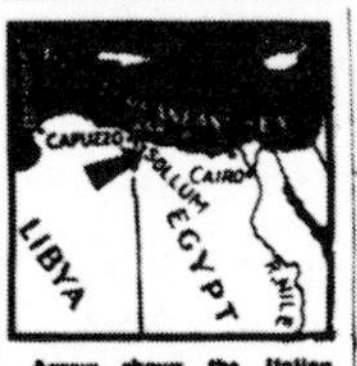

Arrow shows the Italian thrust to occupy Sollum.

CAIRO, Sunday.

"SEVERE handling" of Italian troops moving into Egypt is reported by British G.H.Q. from Cairo to-day.

The communiqué states: "Penetration of the Italian forces into the desert area evacuated by the British continues. Camps are being constructed in the neighbourhood of Birnuh, seven miles south of Sollum.

"The enemy has already exposed himself to severe handling by aircraft and armoured fighting vehicles, and a column ascending to the coastal plain at Halfaya has suffered heavily from artillery fire."

Hammering

"While our casualties continue to be insignificant, there is believed to have lost many men and vehicles.

The R.A.F. is hammering the enemy too. To-day's R.A.F. communiqué says:

"In the West Desert where Italian bombers were active on the night of September 13-14 our bombers made successful attacks on concentrations of enemy motor transports in the Sollum area."

It is not considered here that Italy's occupation of Sollum is of sufficient military importance to bring Egypt into the war.

But, a Government official said to-day should the "Italian action definitely develop into a planned invasion of Egypt, I have no hesitation in saying that we should declare war."

FOOTNOTE from Rome : Official reports in Rome yesterday reported that the Italians hope to reach Alexandria within a minimum and one month or a maximum of two months.—Reuter and B.U.P. messages.

Another Hospital Bombed

PATIENTS SAFE

By Daily Mail Raid Reporter

GERMAN bombers, bound on their nightly terror raiding, arrived at 8.10 last evening.

London's terrific barrage of A.A. guns, stronger than ever at times, forced them to adopt new tactics.

Circling round London at leisure was no longer safe.

Instead, flying at a great height and at top speed they cut straight across London in one direction, scattering bombs as they went.

But there were not many bombs, which, together with the speed of the 'planes, suggested that fast fighters were being used in place of the more vulnerable bombers.

Incendiary bombs were dropped, but watchers reported that up to midnight no fires had been caused. A.R.P. services were evidently working perfectly.

For the first few hours the raiders came at ten-minute intervals.

Once More

Once more the raiders, in their repeated attack on military objectives, bombed a hospital.

One of the oldest of London's hospitals was hit, and a medical block was wrecked.

A high explosive bomb fell right through a staircase in the block, but missed wards on either side. Fortunately the patients had been removed from the wards to basement shelters some time before the gunfire. A doctor was wounded.

As the night wore on the gunfire in central London rose to a crescendo. Bombs fell at a number of points.

In an effort to evade the guns' sound-detector a 'plane glided silently over London with engines cut out, dropped its bombs, and then roared away.

A number of high explosive bombs were dropped in a south-west London district. One bomb demolished two or three houses, and it is feared that there are casualties.

High explosive bombs were dropped on a row of shops in a N.W. district. There were several casualties.

A high explosive bomb hit a large office building in central London early this morning. A fire was started but was quickly put out.

An hotel nearby was shaken by the explosion, but no damage was done.

Marshal is Missing

The "air marshal directing the attacking on Britain," who is reported to have flown over London in Thursday night's raid is now declared to be missing.

This was announced by the German-controlled Paris radio last night. They added that they hoped he was a prisoner.

Hasso von Wedel, crack German pilot and member of Goring's circus in the last war, was shot down by a Hurricane in south-east England yesterday.

As he crashed his machine killed a baby and injured a farmer and his wife. Von Wedel stepped out unhurt.

Leon Blum Arrested

They Battled with Ton Time-bomb

ST. PAUL'S IS SAVED BY SIX HEROES

By Daily Mail Reporter

A LITTLE party of experts—an officer, Lieut. R. Dav_ and five men—have saved St. Paul's Cathedral from almost certain destruction by a gigantic German time-bomb which fell from a 'plane on Thursday and buried itself 26ft. deep in a crater near the walls.

Yesterday at noon, after three days' continuous work, the bomb, 8ft. long, fitted with fuses which made it perilous to handle, was secured by steel tackle and hauled to the surface with a pulley and cable attached to two lorries.

It was one of the biggest that had fallen in London and weighed a ton.

A City fireman who had been on duty continuously in the area told me :

"There were five of them, all young fellows, officered by a French-Canadian. One was an Irishman and a couple came from Yorkshire. Another, I believe, came from Lancashire.

"On the first day they couldn't start work because a six-inch gas-main, broken by the bomb, was blazing. But they've been here from early morning till dusk ever since.

"It was wonderful to watch. They used no scaffolding or supports, and there was a risk of the road falling in at any moment.

"After digging through gravel and sand they came to black mud. The bomb was still slipping along through this almost horizontally, and in 24 hours it would have tunnelled under the Cathedral steps.

"But at last they got it. I heard one of them shout down the crater : 'Have you got it yet ?'—and at last the answer, 'Yes. Here it is ! Listen !'

"The boy down there was ringing his spade against it."

Reinforced

"Then along came more experts. They had to send for three tons of steel tackle before they got it out."

The streets were cleared by the police from St. Paul's to Hackney Marshes. The bomb was placed on a fast lorry and driven away by Lieut. Davies, the risk of explosion being imminent all the time.

Later the bomb was blown up by the bomb disposal section. It caused a 100ft. crater and rattled windows, and in one case loosened plaster, in houses far away on the marshes.

Here is the diary of the bomb.

The bomb whistled to earth at 2.30 a.m. It was discovered at an estimated depth of 15ft. beneath the pavement, almost immediately under the clock-tower on the south-west corner of the Cathedral.

A huge circle of shops, offices, and warehouses round the cathedral were evacuated.

All Friday, Saturday, and Sunday morning the bomb slipped deeper and the men dug. Yesterday morning, 80½-hours after it had fallen, it was safely retrieved.

All that remains in Dean's-court is a deep crater, wide at the surface, narrowing as it deepest to the width of a man's body.

Peering down the crater, with its ominous bend under the steps of the Cathedral, I understood when they said :

"If it weren't for those young sappers the whole front of St. Paul's would have been blown to pieces."

Ten minutes after the bomb had

BACK Page Column FOUR

PALACE BOMBED AGAIN

By Daily Mail Reporter

BUCKINGHAM PALACE was bombed again yesterday for the third time, when two heavy bombs and a number of incendiaries were dropped in a daylight attack.

The King and Queen were not in the palace. The heavy bombs which fell failed to explode—and the raider was shot to pieces by Spitfires a few seconds after the attack.

Only one of the two heavy bombs fell on the palace buildings.

It tore through the ceiling of the Tapestry Room, which is used by the Queen as a drawing-room, on the first floor.

The other fell on the lawns and it and the first one were later exploded by experts. The fire bombs landed in the palace grounds and started small fires on the grass, but these were soon put out.

Part of a bomb-rack was also found in the grounds.

No Evacuation

It was stated unofficially last night that the usual precautions had been taken in the case of bombs that have not exploded. The danger area had been roped off and sandbagged.

The question of any evacuation of the staff, it was stated, did not arise, and it was emphasised that the Royal Family were in the country as usual at week-ends.

The Queen's private suite, damaged yesterday, adjoins the King's apartment, and was formerly used by Queen Mary.

The rooms are on the first floor the north-west wing, overlooking Constitution Hill.

The colour scheme of the rooms is olive green, white, and gold.

Hungarians Accusing Rumania of 'Terror'

BUDAPEST, Sunday.

A SEMI-OFFICIAL statement issued here to-day accuses the Rumanian Army of a 10-day "reign of terror" against Hungarians living in Transylvania and declares that "the crisis between the two countries continues."

Commenting that the part played by the Iron Guard—now in power in Rumania—was "still unclear," the statement says:

Westminster Abbey H_

The west window of West Abbey was slightly damaged on her third air-raid.

The damage was slight and only a few small pane broken, said an official.

The Clare Reported Missing

From Daily Mail Correspondent

NEW YORK, Sunday.—The British flying-boat Clare is missing on her third flight from England to the United States, says the New York Daily News.

"Fear in aviation circles that the machine met with disaster is increased by a wireless message that a 'huge 'plane' was forced down in the Atlantic on Saturday," adds the report.

The Clare, a flying boat of 23 tons, began a weekly passenger and mail service between Britain and New York last month.

On her first Atlantic flight in August her skipper was Capt. J. C. Kelly Rogers, the former Imperial Airways pilot.

LATEST

BERLIN ALARM

Berlin, Monday—An raid alarm was sound in Berlin at 11.30 p.m. ye The All Clear sounded

A second alarm w at 1.55 a.m. to-day. Clear following at Anti-aircraft fire in the city.—B.U.P.

5 KILLED IN ST_

A London hospital by an incendiary bomb yesterday's raid.

Four men and a were killed while wail crowded street in a Wales last night. Bo near the city's shief damaged.

E-BOATS TEST OUR DEFENCE

Towards the end of the month there was a stepping-up of raids upon British factories. There was a damaging raid—90 tons of high explosive and 24 oil-bombs—at the Bristol Aeroplane Company's works at Filton, just outside Bristol.

Then there was a raid upon the Spitfire factory at Southampton. There was not much damage but 100 people were killed. The Germans were now using the Me 109 and Me 110 as a fighter-bomber—a 1914–18 war device which seemed to swing the balance of power in the air-war back into the Luftwaffe's favour.

That didn't last long. On September 27, out of 80 planes heading to bomb Bristol and 300 heading for London, 55 were shot down—compared with the R.A.F.'s 28.

On September 30, 47 Germans were shot down for only 20 British.

General Adolf Galland, one of the German aces, explained: "One of our difficulties was that the fighters had to slow down to keep the bombers covered. Well, we couldn't slow down. We had to zig-zag so that they could keep up with us. That way you used up precious fuel. It was hell being attached to a bomber."

The Luftwaffe had by now lost 25 per cent of its operational strength and a lot of prestige. It tried another tactic: high altitude bombing. Coming in over London at heights of around 20,000 feet. This helped them to confuse radar detection and they couldn't be properly plotted by the Royal Observer Corps.

So Londoners took it . . . and took it. What historians called Phase Five of the Battle of Britain, Cockneys, with their humour, called worse names. The valour of civilians was so great that King George VI announced two decorations for civilians—the George Cross and the George Medal. The George Cross to rank second only to the Victoria Cross.

There seemed little that could be done to beat off the night raiders and the time it took for fighters to climb up to the heights of the bombers was half an hour—a long, vulnerable time in an air-battle.

The British weather, however, helped. On October 12 Hitler, realising that autumn and winter would playh avoc with his invasion plans, postponed Operation Sealion until the spring.

Britain settled down under fire, a fire that blazed most fiercely in London. But, gradually, the British began to realise that they could carry on a nearly-normal life. The nightly moan of the sirens, the regular scuttle to the shelters—these could be fitted into your day almost casually. People talked about the comradeship that the blitz gave them . . . the drawing together of a people in a common danger. Even the King was with them in that danger. Why, hadn't an unexploded landmine landed in *his* back-garden at Buckingham Palace?

Between September 7 and November 13 it was estimated that 160 aircraft bombed London for 67 consecutive nights.

There were moments of comic light relief, even for those R.A.F. fighter pilots whose life span was reckoned to be just over three weeks.

Fighter ace Peter Townsend tells the story of how a Heinkel bomber landed on a British airfield and then—realising its mistake—took off again very quickly. And there was another bomber that crash landed into an airfield. The door opened and the crew tumbled out, inflated

The Battle of Britain nears its end. The Germans, now suffering great losses, step up their attacks on factories in Britain.

their dinghy, got into it—and tried to row away across the field. They thought they'd landed in the sea!

People laughed at stories like these . . . and then gradually realised that they *were* laughing. The tension of the time was relaxing in their minds.

Without realising it, the Battle of Britain was over.

Of course, the raids were to continue, horrifyingly, but it is now known that if any dates can be fixed for the battle they are these—

BEGINNING: July 10
ENDING: October 31

Because what had happened in a period of sixteen weeks was that the might of the Luftwaffe had been challenged and found wanting. There had been no invasion; the Channel had been too much for the Nazis; so had the British people.

In a way the Battle was like a perilous path through a forest that suddenly becomes a wide road. America was to join in the fight against Germany . . . so was Russia. Britain would no longer be alone. As someone said about that night of September 15: "It wasn't the end of the Battle of Britain but it was the beginning of the end." The Battle itself, in relation to the war, was the end of the beginning.

THE REASON WHY

Adolf Hitler, the rumour said, used to chew his carpet every time he lost his temper; his anger was that violent. It was the kind of comedy-propaganda that used to cheer up the Britisher in the blitz-darkened days after the Battle of Britain. Hitler's digestion must have been under a great strain after the Battle of Britain had ended. So great that he turned his attention elsewhere—to attack Russia in June, 1941. The United States came into the war just about six months after that.

For Hitler realised that the Battle of Britain was lost; Britain was the first country in Europe to defy him and live.

Why?

There are many reasons. The initial reason, perhaps, was the foresight of Air Chief Marshal Dowding in writing that May 16 letter asking that no more fighters be sent to France. That foresight and his conduct of Britain's defences during the Battle earned him the Knight Grand Cross of the Order of the Bath on September 30, 1940. He himself has said that not many people realised just how significant the outcome of the Battle would be. He did and his commanders did.

Another reason was the tactics of the Germans. Each time they were on the point of winning some victory they stopped for some reason—like the bombing of our airfields—and Goering might have been a great fighter-ace of the 1914–18 war but he was not gifted with the best of tactical brains. He and his men did not realise the importance of radar which forecast the heavy bomber massings.

That radar, and the way the enemy's moves were plotted by W.A.A.F.s, girls who were prepared to take their place alongside the men. One aircraft woman who was at R.A.F. Tangmere during the Battle was Wing Commander Claire Legge. She said: "During the Battle of Britain the W.A.A.F.s had undoubtedly proved themselves to be hardworking and efficient and would play an increasingly important part in the workings of the Royal Air Force. It was a kind of emancipation."

Another lack on the part of the Nazis was that they had no four-engined heavy bombers which could have saturated Britain. And the bombers that *did* hit Britain failed to recognise the fact that the British under stress became more belligerent. In the bulldog symbol of Winston Churchill they had a leader and a faith to follow that no amount of damaging bombs could dent.

86

There were many other reasons why the British just did not give in . . . the fighter-squadrons from Hitler-conquered countries who found revenge the sweeter while chasing the Germans through British skies. The Poles for instance, often with 500 flying hours—compared to the often "green" British pilots with sometimes ten hours—were at first kept out of the real fights because of the language problem.

But not for long. Dowding wrote to the Air Council in 1941: "I must confess that I had been a little doubtful of the effect which their experience in their own country might have had upon the Polish (and Czech) pilots. But my doubts were laid to rest. The squadrons swung into the fight with a dash and enthusiasm which is beyond praise. They were inspired by a burning hatred for the Germans which made them very deadly opponents. The first Polish Squadron, Number 303, in 11 Group, during the course of a month shot down more Germans than any British unit in the same period."

One of the men at the top who was keeping Fighter Command equipped with planes was Lord Beaverbrook, then Minister of Aircraft Production. In the three weeks just before and during Dunkirk, Fighter Command had lost fifty per cent of its then front-line strength in aircraft. Often aircraft arrived at airfields without guns, non-operational—hard work for those ground crews without whom the pilots could not have been airborne.

Beaverbrook changed all that. Planes arrived ready to fight and the numbers and quality improved.

His son, Sir Max Aitken, said: "I've never seen a man work so hard. His eyes were bloodshot and they were crying with the strain; *he* wasn't crying, his eyes were. He was working a seven-day week and eighteen hours during a day. He drove himself and everybody else."

Sir Max was one of those for whom Beaverbrook was driving himself. Four hundred and forty-three R.A.F. pilots were killed out of the 2,400 who fought in the Battle, and sixty-four air gunners, navigators and radar operators were killed and another fifty or so were wounded out of 600.

They were called Knights of the Sky who sacrificed themselves for Britain. But they themselves had little use for mock-heroics.

Said Aitken: "There was the constant sense of being tired. There were no heroics—you were just doing a job. But you had to do that job professionally because you were up against professionals."

He spoke about the loneliness of the dogfight. Those dogfights might be thought of as knightly jousts by those watching from below. But as one writer put it: "It was the one form of war in which the object was to catch your enemy unaware, from behind, and shoot him in the back. All other tactics stemmed from this."

Adolf Galland, for the Germans, thought that it was "a hard battle, a tough, nasty battle—but fair in so far as it was man against man. Goering once said to me: 'What would your reaction be if you were asked to shoot somebody on the end of a parachute?' I said: 'I am prepared to fight but that would be murder.'

"There was a pause for four to five seconds then Goering said: 'You are right: I would not have done it in the 1914–18 war.

"But you had to try to kill the pilot in that machine, because he was more important than the plane. Always the element of surprise—that is what you aimed for."

Then Galland laughed. "But you had to take care not to come too near to the plane you were firing at. Otherwise the bullets would rebound at you."

The Intelligence reports received by the Germans rebounded as well. They were always incredibly exaggerated. On October 3, 1940, the people of Germany were told in a radio broadcast: "London is facing riots, the authorities prove to be helpless and everywhere there is violent confusion."

It was the Nazis who were confused. As an Australian newspaper, the Sydney *Morning Herald*, said on September 12, 1940: "London and England can endure the worse cruelties that it is within Hitler's power to wreak. Britain's resistance will certainly not be weakened by this mass murder of civilians.

"Stubborn will and growing might are rendering the tyrant desperate. The deeper he steeps his country in blood-guilt, the greater will be the accumulation of world hatred against his gangster regime and the more terrible will be the reckoning in the end."

What would have happened if Hitler had invaded? Sir Max Aitken said: "If the Germans had managed to ground the R.A.F. they would have come over. And if they had come over they would have captured Southern England. What then?

"I suppose we would have retreated and gone behind the Welsh mountains; you just can't tell what would have happened. The Royal Family would have had to be moved and so on.

"Some of the spirit would have gone out of the country. If the Germans had got tanks ashore on the South Coast it would have been terribly dangerous for us."

Then he nutshelled why the Battle of Britain was so important: "Our winning the Battle of Britain prevented that."

If . . .

If Dowding had not written that letter . . .

If Goering had pressed on bombing British airfields . . .

If the Luftwaffe had not switched to blitz British cities . . .

If the British R.A.F. pilot had not been the kind of fighter he was . . .

You can play the "If" game with history and life. In the end you find that things came out the way they did for simple reasons, often hidden by the events of the time.

The Times newspaper looked back on that time in 1942 and said: "All that was left of freedom in Europe was at bay on British soil."

The Battle of Britain was to merge into the Allies' further victories which were to lead to the end of World War Two in 1945.

But for sixteen weeks in 1940 Britain was alone. It was a time for heroes without heroics, for courage without thought, for valour without medals. People hardly even knew when the Battle of Britain ended . . . But, during those sixteen weeks in 1940, a world had been saved and young men had gone out to die for freedom.

It was a brave summer.

A German fighter cork-
screwing to the ground
after a direct hit by a
Spitfire.

BUILD UP OF BATTLE

On June 18, 1940 Prime Minister Winston Churchill broadcast to the British people. He gave a name to the summer months of combat that were soon to follow. "What General Weygand called the Battle of France is over; the Battle of Britain is about to begin."

What led up to that Battle and what led from that Battle is here briefly delineated.

The terseness of these entries can only imply the danger and perils of that hour, an hour that Prime Minister Churchill was to call Britain's "Finest".

February 26 1935	Hitler officially creates German Luftwaffe with Hermann Goering as Commander-in-Chief.
July 14 1936	British Fighter Command formed with Air Chief Marshal Sir Hugh Dowding as Air Officer Commanding-in-Chief.
September 1 1939	Germany invades Poland. Second World War begins.
September 3 1939	Britain declares war on Germany.
May 10 1940	Neville Chamberlain resigns as Prime Minister. Winston Churchill becomes Britain's Prime Minister.
May 16 1940	Air Chief Marshal Dowding's historic letter expressing grave concern at denuding Britain by sending fighters to France.
June 4 1940	Churchill says: "We shall fight on the beaches, we shall fight on the landing grounds, we shall fight in the fields and in the streets, we shall fight in the hills; we shall never surrender."
June 18 1940	Hitler to Goering: "The war is finished. I'll come to an understanding with England."
June 22 1940	Signing of Franco-German Armistice. According to Gallup Poll only three per cent of British population believe war might be lost. In America thirty-two per cent of the population expect British victory but thirty-three per cent are uncertain.
July 10 1940	**THE BATTLE OF BRITAIN BEGINS.**

ly 10-August 7	Phase One of the Battle of Britain: attacks on coastal shipping.
ly 16 1940	Hitler's Directive 16, designating preparations for a landing operation against England—Operation Sealion.
ly 19 1940	Goering is raised to Reichmarschall of Germany.
ly 19 1940	Hitler addresses the Reichstag: " . . . I feel it to be my duty before my own conscience to appeal once more to reason and common sense in Great Britain . . . I consider myself in a position to make this appeal, since I am not a vanquished foe begging favours, but the victor, speaking in the name of reason. I can see no reason why this war need go on."
ly 22 1940	Lord Halifax rejects Hitler's peace terms. Paul Baudouin, French Foreign Minister, says: " . . . if the Germans do not master England this autumn, they will have lost the war."
ly 31 1940	"The air war will start now and will determine our ultimate relative strength . . ." Adolf Hitler.
gust 1 1940	Hitler's Directive 17 for the combat of air and sea warfare against England.
ugust 8-23 1940	Phase Two of the Battle of Britain. Radar stations and airfields under attack.
ugust 13 1940	Eagle Day. German total strength exceeds 2,550 planes immediately serviceable. Fighter Command can muster 749 fighters.
ugust 15 1940	Goering calls off attacks on radar sites "in view of the fact that not one of those attacked had so far been put out of action."
ugust 24 1940	German bombers accidentally drop bombs on London.
ugust 24-Sept. 6	Phase Three of the Battle of Britain. Attacks on airfields intensified.
ugust 25/26 1940	As a result of German attack on London Winston Churchill orders reprisal raid of 81 bombers on Berlin.
ptember 4 1940	At the Sportspalast in Berlin, Hitler announces that, "If they attack our cities we will simply erase theirs."
pt. 7-Nov. 3	Average of 200 German bombers attack London every night.
ptember 7-30	Phase Four of the Battle of Britain. The Blitz begins.
ptember 7 1940	Goering publicly assumes command of air warfare.
pt. 14 1940	Hitler postpones Operation Sealion (the invasion of Britain) for three days.
pt. 15 1940	Marked climax of aerial conflict when Luftwaffe suffered heaviest losses. First reports indicated that 175 German planes had been shot down. This was optimistic. Celebrated as **BATTLE OF BRITAIN DAY.**

Sept. 17 1940	Operation Sealion is postponed indefinitely.
October 1-31 1940	Phase Five of the Battle of Britain. High altitude daylight bombing. Night bombing continues.
October 12 1940	Operation Sealion is called off until following Spring.
October 31-onwards	Night attacks on cities continues—The Blitz—but daylight attack diminish.
	THE BATTLE OF BRITAIN IS WON.

The Author of the *Battle of Britain book*

TOM HUTCHINSON was born in Sheffield, Yorkshire, in 1930, and remembers little about the battle—apart from the blitzes which hit the steel city during the war.

He started work as a reporter on the *Sheffield Telegraph* before moving to London to work on such publications as *Kinematograph Weekly*, *Picturegoer* and *Illustrated*. He later joined ABC TV as scriptwriter of their religious programmes, while writing for such programmes as "This Week". He was with the *Daily Express* before moving to Tyne Tees Television for three years as producer-scriptwriter on documentaries.

On his return to London he took up a similar appointment with ITN and freelanced for numerous major magazines and newspapers, before becoming film critic and then Features Editor of *Nova* magazine.

Tom Hutchinson lives in Highgate Village, London, with his wife and two sons, Michael and Stephen. His hobbies include the cinema and his stereo record collection.

Research Assistant for the *Battle of Britain book*

JILL THOMAS was educated at Hawnes School in Bedford and at Millfield, Somerset, and she spent several months studying in Florence, Italy, a visit which coincided with the floods which severely damaged famous art treasures.

Before working on the *Battle of Britain* film (and carrying out research for this book), she also worked on other films—notably the "Carry On . . ." pictures. Her interests are the cinema and fast cars.

AUTHOR'S ACKNOWLEDGEMENTS

To write a book like this means that you have not only to talk to the people who were involved in such a struggle, but . . . to read other books.

Bishop, Edward. *Their Finest Hour—The Story of the Battle of Britain 1940*. Ballantine Books, 1968.
Clark, Ronald W. *Battle for Britain*. George G. Harrap & Co. Ltd., 1965.
McKee, Alexander. *Strike from the Sky—The Battle of Britain Story*. Souvenir Press Ltd., 1960; paperback ed., New English Library, 1969.
Narracott, A. H. *In Praise of the Few*. Frederick Muller Ltd., 1947.
Wood, Derek, and Dempster, Derek. *The Narrow Margin*. Hutchinson & Co. Ltd., 1961; paperback ed., Arrow Books Ltd., 1967.

I'm sure I've missed some of the books; some unconsciously, some have disappeared into the limbo of time. Anyway, to whoever, whatever, wherever—thank you!

Grateful acknowledgement is made to the following:

Collins, Publishers, for permission to use an extract from *1940* by Laurence Thompson; John Farquharson Ltd. and Hodder and Stoughton Limited for permission to use an extract from *Nine Lives* by Al Deere; Leslie Frewin Publishers Ltd. for permission to use an extract from *The Wit of Sir Winston* compiled by Adam Sykes and Iain Sproat; George C. Harrap & Company Limited for permission to use an extract from *Battle for Britain* by Ronald W. Clark; the Imperial War Museum for permission to reproduce the poster on p. 17; Macmillan & Co. Ltd. for permission to use an extract from *The Last Enemy* by Richard Hillary; the Estate of Edward R. Murrow for permission to use an extract from a broadcast by the late Mr. Murrow; Michael Joseph Ltd. for permission to use an extract from *The Hurricane Story* by Paul Gallico; Cassell & Co. Ltd. for permission to use extracts from *The War Speeches of Sir Winston Churchill*, Vol. 1; Robert Hale Ltd. for permission to use an extract from *Ginger Lacey— Fighter Pilot* by Richard Townsend Bickers.